PREPARING FOR THE JUNGLE

AVOIDING SNAKES & PITFALLS ON THE PATH TO HEALTHY LOVE

Tamara Kiekhaefer, LCSW

Post Hill
PRESS

A POST HILL PRESS BOOK
ISBN: 978-1-63758-253-4
ISBN (eBook): 978-1-63758-254-1

Cover design by Tiffani Shea
Interior design by Yoni Limor

Editing by Bonnie Hearn Hill
Workbook inserts by Ma Cristina Baldovino
Organizational development by Christine Aguilar and Ian
Gordon of Aguilar-Gordon Consulting

Post Hill Press
New York • Nashville
posthillpress.com

Published in the United States of America
1 2 3 4 5 6 7 8 9 10

Testimonials for Tamara Kiekhaefer

"Through working with Tami, I found the courage to leave a toxic relationship as well as the strength to move forward and find myself again. Every step of the way, she has offered personalized attention, thoughtful perspectives, and helpful tools to guide me in the process. I could not be more happy with the direction that I'm headed in and I'm so grateful for her influence in my life!"

—J.T.

"Due to a variety of reasons, I've always used dating and relationships as a way to fill voids. Working with Tami and the help and guidance she provided, it took a lot of time, self-reflection, and interpersonal focus to even realize this was a pattern for me. However, once I recognized this and put in the effort to figure out why I had these 'voids,' where they were originating from, why I felt the need to fill them etc. I was able to address them in a healthy way. I believe that once you're operating from a state of wholeness it's extremely empowering to know you have the ability to make healthy dating choices. You grow courage and confidence to walk away from someone giving you mixed signals, and you actually feel proud for doing so! Whereas before you would probably doubt yourself, feel insecure, and actually let their mixed signals influence how you felt about yourself. Ultimately, I think it's life changing—you allow yourself to change your perspective of what you're willing to entertain/accept and it gives you the strength to walk away from red flags and see that as a win! Tami was and still is instrumental in the growth I experience in this area!"

—**M.W.**

"When I first started seeing Tami, to say I was not in the best place would be an understatement. I had just gotten out of a two-and-a-half year relationship that didn't quite end the way that I thought it would, and I spent the majority of my days just trying to make it through without crying and ruminating about where it all went wrong. Fast forward two years later, Tami has not only supported me through one of the most emotional times in my life to-date, but has helped me get back out in the dating scene with a newfound confidence and understanding of what I will, and will not, settle for—and I know this is just the beginning of my revamped view of relationships. So thank you Tami, I appreciate you more than you know!"

—**A.W.**

"Tami helped me move forward from a long term abusive relationship by working with me to realize my self-worth, establish what I wanted in future relationships, and learn how to identify red flags as I reentered the dating world. All of this work prepared me to be ready to meet and commit to my current boyfriend in a wonderful and healthy relationship."

—**L.N.**

DEDICATION

This book is dedicated to all the men who broke my heart, taught me lessons of what I didn't want in a relationship, and helped me turn inward to uncover the empowered woman I am today.

Table of Contents

INTRODUCTION:
It's a Jungle Out There

WHETHER YOU'RE GETTING READY to explore the dating world, or you're already in a romantic relationship and feeling unfulfilled, or you just need to touch up a few areas, this book will be your guide. The process of internal change requires you to get messy and experiment with different ways of thinking, feeling, and behaving. Changing habits means challenging yourself to get out of your comfort zone because comfort doesn't always mean healthy. Once you have finished this book, you will better understand what is in the jungle—the plethora of personalities, cultures, and styles that frequently confuse and overwhelm us—as well as your place in that jungle.

You've experienced the awkward first date, the unsettled third date, wondering where this whole thing is headed. Then, a couple weeks or months in, you're wondering if you should broach the subject of exclusivity. After all the head-spinning internal conversation as you try to figure the situation out, you find out that you must have missed the blazing red flags of toxicity and doom: your phone is no longer ringing, and text messages go silent. *Damn it! What happened?* you ask yourself. *Was I unattractive, boring, overbearing?*

What happened is very simple: you were not prepared for the jungle.

I don't have to tell you it's a jungle out there because that's probably the reason—at least one of the reasons—you picked up this book. I'm guessing you've explored that dating jungle and have had romantic interactions that left you with only question marks and scars. As you already know, the jungle is a vibrant atmosphere where all kinds of people live. They are mysterious, dignified, ruthless, wild, fresh, muddy, and perfectly imperfect. And yes, that includes you too. In order to create healthy loving relationships, strong, sturdy friendships, or reliable, secure work relationships, you must address the deep and dark parts of yourself—the unexamined wilderness of your past—so that you can stabilize your present and prepare for your future. I will help you do that.

Throughout these chapters, I'll coach you to gain the tools, mindset, belief system, and confidence necessary to succeed in the jungle so that when you open your door to venture out, you'll be fully prepared to get out there. If you are dating around, you'll be ready to find a healthy, lasting, loving relationship with a person who is available to give and receive exactly what you're looking for. If you're already in a relationship, you'll have the tools to set boundaries, communicate effectively, and ask for what you need. You will be able to strengthen your relationship because you will have tapped into your inner strength with the utmost respect for yourself, your partner, and the relationship.

ABOUT ME

Not only have I had a private practice for twenty years and helped thousands of adults and couples with relationships, but I have experienced heartache, loneliness, sadness, the feeling of giving up, being guarded, being too passive, hating who I was, and feeling like nothing was ever going to change. I got to a point where I was tired of the way my relationships had been my whole life. I figured out how to change. So can you.

Here is how I know that this program works: In high school and college, I placed my sense of self in the hands of men. If they gave me attention, I felt on top of the world. If they turned their attention elsewhere, I felt completely rejected. My confidence was tied to a yo-yo, and I lost all control of my self-worth and self-respect. My first real relationship was in college with a guy who lived four states away. I attended Colorado State University, but I fell in love on a spring break trip in California. We actually made it work until I graduated from college when we went from long distance to moving in together. That lasted six months, and I moved out.

Quickly after that, I met a guy who was my colleague at a juvenile correction facility. That was a rollercoaster ride. At first, it was incredible: Sparks and extremes on every level. Never a dull moment. Amazing sex. But then the jealousy started, accompanied by controlling behavior, erratic moods. As happens in such cycles, he'd be really nice, and I'd forgive him, until he would mistreat me again. Months and years of this passed, behaviors just got worse, and my confidence tanked. I finally moved back to Colorado to get away. That's when I met the man I later married.

He was 180 degrees opposite the last relationship. When I met my husband, I realized that I was seeking a stable, predictable, you-know what-the-rest-of-your-life-will-look-like type of love. We were really good for a while. But as the years went by, I realized I had morphed into what I thought he wanted me to be. I had lost my sparkle: my need to live and think outside the box. My need to chase my dreams with my hair on fire. The more I took action steps to make these seemingly impossible dreams a reality, the more I think I freaked him out. I started teaching yoga, I vacationed alone, I even went as far as trying to plan a fundraiser for the Wounded Warrior Project, which would have been a Toby Keith concert at the Air Force Academy. My hair was blazing at this point, and I damn near pulled off that concert event! My husband would ask why I needed to rock the boat, got angry that I was focusing on ridiculous ideas, and eventually thought I was out of my mind. Which maybe I was, but I was also coming out of my damn skin. We finally decided that neither one of us was happy, and we were just too different. We also completely lacked the communication skills required to make our marriage work. We communicated less and less and eventually grew too far apart to ever get back on the same page. We have two amazing kids, and we do well as co-parents.

After that, I knew I had to figure out this whole "relationship" thing. And I did it by setting out to find me. When I did the work—the hard, grueling, look-in-the-mirror type work—I figured it out. I understood all the aspects that were so necessary for me to be a complete me. That's when I met Jim.

He's not too far to one side or the other. Like a pendulum, he falls exactly in the middle, the perfect landing spot for me. We fight, but we fight fair; we communicate. And after a fight, I feel closer to him because we hold that space for each other. He encourages me to dream and to chase my passions. We have respect for each other. These are skills you will learn too.

I have found love again and know this will be my person to grow old with. I want to show you how to find your person.

HOW TO USE THIS BOOK

The book is formatted into sections for a reason. As we go through the step-by-step process, I encourage you to not blaze through it as if your hair were on fire. Spend time. You are worth it. Allow each section to resonate and sink in. Do the work. Allow time between each chapter, so the information and action steps can become part of the new habits you are forming throughout the book.

You will be challenged: you may experience deeper emotions of elation, sadness, and fear, and sometimes traumatic memories may be triggered. We will be examining the past, family dynamics, and former relationships, which can be difficult to bring to the surface. If you're having a difficult time emotionally, mentally, or physically, consider reaching out to a doctor or therapist to help you on an individual basis, as this book is not intended to take the place of psychotherapy and is not intended to diagnose any mental conditions or symptoms. You may use it in conjunction with psychotherapy to gain more understanding of your specific situation.

That being said, roll up your sleeves, grab your pen and paper, and get ready to dig in! Opportunity awaits. I wish you strength, light, and love as you work your way to an empowered space!

I've got you! Let's go!

CHAPTER 1:
Setting Your Intention

WORLD CLASS! YOU ARE going to be world class. Think about it. Ask yourself, *How can I be the best I can be?* Well, what you put into it is what you are going to get out of it.

Where do I start, you ask? Let me introduce you to who I will call Emma. I had seen Emma as a client on and off over the last decade. When I first met Emma, she was just graduating from high school and planning to travel the world before beginning college. She came to therapy because she needed guidance after a boyfriend had broken her heart. Emma was driven and intelligent, and she had the potential to reach any goal she set for herself, but as a young adult, she still had so much to learn about honoring herself; young love is tough and has a way of really messing with your confidence.

In our sessions, she dealt with the pain of the lost teenage relationship, and before I knew it, she was off on her traveling adventures. But after she came back, she continued to pop in and out of therapy over the next few years, calling it her "life tune-up," and I watched her grow as an individual. Over the time we spent together, we worked through career goals, family issues, grief, loss, and, of course, several relationships and broken hearts.

I have a theory I call the "second puberty" (as if anyone wants to go through that twice). The first puberty is the normal puberty we experience in our pre-teenage to mid-teenage years: crazy hormones, pimples, body changing like crazy. The second puberty is between the ages of twenty-one and twenty-eight years old. The changes I see people endure over this time—especially around romantic love—are truly astonishing. Most of us can look back at the relationships we were in—or, in my case, the hopeless crushes I based my poems on—during our early twenties and say, "Thank God that didn't work out! What did I even see in that person?" So yes, there are some examples of high school sweethearts who ended up getting married, having kids, and living happily ever after. But for the most part, who you were attracted to in your early twenties is very different from who you are attracted to in your late twenties.

What is responsible for this radical shift? Well, in Emma's case, she was young, and she didn't stop to think about self-worth, self-love, and self-respect. I mean, who has time for that when you're a teenager and think you already know all the answers to life's problems? But what happened, what resulted in Emma on my couch, was that she hadn't had enough life experience to use as an example of what worked in a relationship and what didn't. She was still in the data-collecting stage of life.

Emma later told me about a man she met while volunteering in an overseas organization. She was sure he was the one, until he cheated on her. And then there was a guy she met in grad school, one she dreamed of having a family with, until she realized he was emotionally unavailable. By the time Emma was thirty years old and sitting in my office, I could see she had completed her second puberty. She was showing up world class.

She had gained useful tools from both therapy and her life experiences and had not only put these tools in her toolkit but begun to implement them in her everyday life. She learned to ask for what she wanted, set firm boundaries with others, trust her intuition, and make sure that she was a priority in her own life. She was now at a place where her personality was generally the same as when I met her, but her values and priorities had shifted. Her perspective on life issues had matured.

When people speak of having a mid-life crisis, it is sort of the same thing. However, I think people have several of these "crises" throughout their lives. I have one every seven to eight years. Think about this in your own life: Can you see where things took a major shift every several years? Maybe it was a job change, a relationship change, a move, a new hobby, new friendships, new activities?

Most people tend to notice this change only when it's a tsunami of a shift, but small changes happen all the time. They may make you panic, but if you recognize the rolling waves of transformation as opportunity, they aren't as scary. Sometimes the changes are positive, and sometimes they are painful. Sometimes they are influenced by other people, and sometimes we initiate the changes. Sometimes they are minor, and other times, they bowl you over. But every time, change is an opportunity to learn and grow.

I love getting check-ins from Emma, even if it's a Christmas card, because when I think of world class, I think of her. She has taken the time to do the hard work and become so completely empowered in her life.

It takes determination and commitment to be world class. I have been providing psychotherapy for another client—I'll call her Lucy—for about two years. She came to me after a minor surgery went horribly wrong: she went septic and almost died. Prior to the surgery, Lucy was an athlete, running marathons and lifting weights. After the surgery, her life changed dramatically. Requiring a colostomy bag and enduring additional surgeries, her body looked different, scarred by incisions. Her level of depression, anxiety, and post-traumatic stress was ruining her life. But she was able to endure by exercising physical strength and mental toughness. Throughout our time working together, she never wavered from her focus. Of course, there were occasional meltdowns, but after allowing herself to feel the emotion and work through the pain, she would scrape herself together and get back to the fight of recovery. Today, her body is stronger than ever, and she is back to running marathons. Her mind is sharp, and she has learned to manage the anxiety.

Despite the setbacks of unexpected ER visits and emergency surgeries, her spirit is dynamic as her confidence continues to flourish. Due to this determination and commitment, Lucy's personal trainers and doctors have been astonished at the progress she has made. This would not have been possible if she didn't execute the consistent effort required from within. Her story continues to inspire me.

Do you have to endure trauma like Lucy or Emma in order to become world class? Absolutely not. However, you do have to tap into their mindsets and be willing to play the long game, not the short game, for lasting results. The goal is to dial into what you really want, your impact on others, and how you live day to day. By doing that, you will cultivate a vision of the future.

It took you this long to create habits that don't serve you; it will take some time to relearn habits that will result in positive outcomes. You will have to work hard, but be patient with yourself. Having a daily routine is your foundation: it will allow you to increase your creativity, energy, and motivation. If you have that foundation, everything you learn in this book will be built on solid ground. I will now guide you on how to establish this routine.

First and foremost, you must get your mind right. Why are you here? Why are you reading this book today? Maybe you want to be happy in your relationship. Maybe you want to meet the person of your dreams. But why? What is that really going to do for you? Let's say it all works out. You spend the time, the energy, the investment. You're in love. You feel stable and content.

What's the point? Are you hoping someone will come along and make you happy? Are you banking on someone else in order to feel fulfilled in your life? Stop relying on someone else to do that for you. No one can. You are responsible for your own happiness. Only when you feel fulfilled inside are you available to share your life with someone else. Remember my morphing example in my marriage? Having your mind right, your foundation established, will allow you to maintain what is important to you, therefore, showing up whole and world class in a relationship. Let's develop your foundation now.

First, you must build the strongest, healthiest relationship with yourself, or any other relationship you attempt to build may crumble. Being world class is about creating the foundation that is required to achieve higher connections.

This vision of what being world class looks like—strength, determination, perseverance, dedication—that I am asking you to create is what will give you the motivation, the gumption, and the determination you will need to work through this book. We are going to talk about some challenging things. I'm going to ask you to carve out time and dedicate it to focusing on yourself. We all have busy lives, but this vision of why you're here today will make you want to show up, pull out your journal, carve out the time, and devote yourself, world-class style.

First, I will introduce you to the Whole Life Grid. Second, I will help you fill out the Grid, and lastly, I will guide you through creating and mastering a routine that will provide stability and structure as you challenge your internal self throughout this book.

Pretend that you fall asleep one night. Your head hits the pillow, and you drift off into this sleep of pure, deep peace. When you wake up, you feel amazing. You feel clear-minded and determined. You are exactly where you want to be in your life. What does this look like? This Whole Life Grid provides you with nine squares, one square for each area of your life. This is your guide to begin doing some brainstorming. In your mind, visualize where you would like to be in six months. What month is it for you now as you read this book? What month is it in six months? What will the weather feel like? Will you most likely be inside, outside, working hard, on vacation? Really get the vision of what this typical month looks like for you. Now, look at each square and write some notes about where you want to be in six months. For example, your alone/spiritual time. What does this mean to you? If you were to develop a vision for this area, what would it look like? How about recreation? What does each square mean to you?

Now, dig in a little more and ask yourself this question: *if I were to feel solid in each of these areas, what would this look like?* Now, before you get too overwhelmed, slow it down a bit! I am giving you permission right now to dream. You're allowed to get creative and dream about what it would feel like to be secure, grounded, and totally at peace in each of these areas. What you are doing right now is training your brain to get what you want. You have probably already mastered the art of talking yourself out of what you want or telling yourself one hundred reasons why your goals or visions are impossible. I am asking you to shift your thinking. Break the habits that do not serve you. Unlock your vision. Unlock the steps to get there.

You want it? You are so much closer than you were yesterday. Yesterday you were still having the conversation that it was impossible. Today, you are considering that there might be a chance. Filling out the Grid doesn't happen in one sitting. This is a work in progress. Do one quick brain dump, take a break, and come back to it. As you return, your vision will solidify.

WHOLE LIFE GRID

WORK	FAMILY	FRIENDS
PRIMARY RELATIOSNHIP	ALONE/ SPIRITUAL	PERSONAL GROWTH
RECREATION	HOBBIES	SERVICE/ GIVING BACK

FIRST ACTION STEP: THE WHOLE LIFE GRID

Now you will shift the thinking and put this into action. Okay, you have your Grid. This is your life separated into nine areas. Instead of taking your entire life on in one sitting and hoping things change, this is a strategic method that allows your brain to chunk your life into smaller areas by gaining a clear understanding of what will make you feel content. Let me explain.

Next, pick one square. Just one. Say you choose "Recreation." Maybe you want to take a trip to Africa, go on a safari, see the national parks, ride an elephant. Is it in the cards for you to drop everything immediately, quit your job, jump on a plane, and climb on an elephant? Probably not. If you remind yourself that you can't do that tomorrow, you shut the dream down. Instead, start where you are and be realistic. Get your brain and your heart in line with your vision. Reframe the way you think about achievement. Really feel this energy. You have choices, and you can create this. Maybe you start by cutting pictures out of a magazine about Africa and all its opportunities. Then, you may take a trip to the zoo. Take in everything, the sights, the smells, and get your mind in a place where you believe you will accomplish this vision. Imagine how you will feel when you are riding the elephant with the wind in your hair. By doing this exercise, you are shifting the idea of *this is impossible* into, *if I really want something in my life, I can work hard, plan, and make it happen.* You are identifying what is important to you and setting short-term, realistic goals to achieve it. Confidence is growing.

Pour your heart into the Grid and spend some time on it over the next week. Allow your mind to rest, and then work a bit, and then rest again.

You are going to own this feeling of being your best, being world class. Because when you feel world class within yourself, a relationship with someone is a bonus. You are just fine already. No one is completing you (although I loved *Jerry Maguire*). They are only complementing you. Whether it is a friendship, a work relationship, or an acquaintance, when you are world class, you will show up ready to establish what is healthy, solid, and grounded.

SECOND ACTION STEP: REFLECT

Grab your journal. Now collect all of your thoughts in detail. I want you to define the different types of relationships you seek to improve. Are you expanding your social circle and want more solid friendships? Are you looking for a romantic relationship or trying to improve the one you have? Maybe you are working on the relationship with yourself and seeking to feel more empowered and connected.

You see, it's not just what the relationship looks like. It's also how you show up. How do you feel? How are you conducting your life, job, day, kids, if you have them? Are you making time for yourself? How would you know if you were happy in your life, with or without a relationship? Where do you find your peace? The first Action Step will give you space to write out what you really want in your relationship. In the second Action Step, you will describe in detail the relationship you have with yourself and the relationships you want with others. It will be interesting to revisit this page after you have completed the last chapter in this book to see if your perspectives or visions shifted at all.

Module 1-
MASTERING YOUR ROUTINE
Your 6 Daily Actions...

"It's not what you do that defines you...
...it's what you do DAILY that defines you."

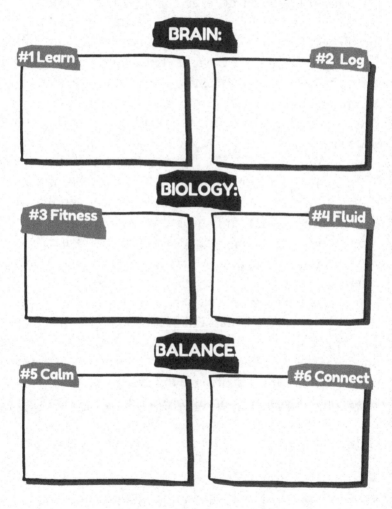

BRAIN:

#1 Learn

#2 Log

BIOLOGY:

#3 Fitness

#4 Fluid

BALANCE

#5 Calm

#6 Connect

THIRD ACTION STEP: MASTER YOUR ROUTINE

Here you will see three sections with two parts to each section: your Brain, your Biology, and your Balance. These three areas and their counterparts encompass every part of your routine to focus on. Here, you will create your non-negotiables—things you do every day, no matter what. The consistency will help you create a routine and set you up for success! You know as you get busy, these daily habits are likely to fall to the wayside. Life happens. But do you know that feeling of butterflies in your stomach, that overwhelming feeling of everything-is-crashing-in-on-me? The irritability, lack of patience with others, snappy tone? So often, this is a sign that you are not making yourself a priority. Your Brain, Biology, and Balance areas have slid to the bottom of the totem pole, and you have become frazzled. You find that your patience is thin, and you may feel more disorganized. Your body is always talking to you and if you pay close attention and take action to practice self-care, you can head off negative outcomes. This structure allows you to stay focused. Here are six things to do every day.

Start with the Brain. You have to take care of the noggin. Here, you see two activities. First, **learn** something new every day. This core curriculum will provide plenty of learning opportunities! Challenge your brain to exercise. Stay sharp up top. The second activity is to **log** every day. As suggested, you should have your journal so you can log your process as you work through this book. It could also be your accountability journal to make sure you are maintaining a routine. Your journal serves as a place and time to get what is in your mind out onto paper. Maybe you log about what is going on in the world, or maybe you log random thoughts you have. On other days, the journal entry will be deep as you process what you are learning about yourself throughout these chapters. Other days, logging may just be the date and "Hi, I don't have much to say. Love, me." (I always end my journal entry with "Love, me." It's my own little hug to myself. Try it out!) Logging will help you retain all your aha moments.

Next is Biology. **Fitness** is doing something to stretch or move your body every day. By being active, you will feel an increase in energy and improvement in sleep. You may even feel a boost in your mood. I've always thought exercise is one of the best medicines for anxiety and depression. You may not do a full workout every day; sometimes, you may just have time to take the stairs or park farther away, requiring you to move the body. This is still great.

Fluid is also part of biology. Also scientifically proven, drinking water provides hundreds of benefits to the body. Experts attest that by the time you feel thirsty, you are already dehydrated. Dehydration sneaks up on you quickly, so making fluid a part of your daily routine creates a healthy habit.

The third area of your routine is Balance. Do something every day to find **calm** and to connect with others. Slowing down your brain by just sitting down, closing your eyes, and paying attention to your breath does wonders throughout the day. **Connecting** with people creates balance. Stop mindlessly scrolling through social media, turn off the TV, and do what you can to engage with other people. If you talk with others on the phone, do exactly that. Talk with them. Don't multitask so you are only partially available.

An app I found that does a great job of tracking these areas is "Done." This will help you categorize, track, and remember to focus on these six areas: Learn, Log, Fitness, Fluid, Calm, and Connect. You can set reminders for yourself, and you'll feel great checking off each one. Play around with the app or create a system that works for you.

MODULE 7-
INSPECTION CHECK LIST

 Respect

 Morals/Values

 Self-Reflection

 Accountable for Actions

 Chemistry

 Trustworthy

 Energy

 Communication Skills

 Attitude

Confidence

COMPLETING A SELF-ASSESSMENT

How do you know what to improve if you don't know what to enhance? Why would you fix something if you didn't think it was broken? Do you feel like a hot mess, but you aren't sure where to even begin to sort yourself out? I have ten areas that I will ask you to reflect on as of today, right now. Not where you think you should be and not where you think other people think you should be. But try to be as honest and straightforward with yourself as you can regarding where you are today. It is too common for us to morph into what we think we need to be, act, say, and do in order to fit into society. But here, as we work together, allow yourself to just be authentic. You, me, that's it. Having a glass of wine and chatting about your life.

At the end of this book, I will reference these ten areas and ask you to reevaluate where you are. I think you will be amazed at the growth and realizations that will be right in front of you. You have the ability inside yourself to show up in your life and check off all ten of the items listed here. Only when you doubt yourself, talk negatively, and focus on the failures do cobwebs cover the potential for you to demonstrate your world-class nature. I encourage you to elaborate in your journal, using this checklist as an internal assessment. Here is a start.

Respect: How are you showing yourself respect? What can you do today to be more respectful to yourself?

Self-reflection: What are your goals? What are your successes?

Chemistry: Are you physically attracted to others? Do you know the type of person you are drawn to based on looks, demeanor? Are you a sexual being? Are you comfortable with intimacy?

Energy: Do you transmit an inviting or uninviting flow? Do you vibe with people around you? Do you draw people toward you or push people away?

Attitude: Are you optimistic, pessimistic, realistic? Is the glass half-full or half-empty? Do you radiate positivity? Gratitude? Non-judgment? Do you bring others down by creating negativity?

Morals/Values: Are you walking your walk and talking your talk? When self-reflecting, are you in line with your beliefs and living your life that way?

Accountable for actions: Do you sincerely apologize for what is yours to own? Do you hold others accountable?

Trustworthy: Do you follow through on commitments? Can people rely on you? Are you honest with yourself?

Communication skills: Do you know your Communication Style? Are you aware when you are disconnected from the people around you? Are you able to adjust in order to work with people? Are you shut down? How do you feel about conflict? What are you doing to be more effective in this area?

Confidence: Do you know your worth? Do you emanate humility? Are you able to comfortably spend time alone?

Focusing on getting your mind, body, and soul prepared is crucial. I know you want to jump in and get going on creating healthy relationships and feeling empowered. But you have tried that before, and it didn't work out. Why? Because you weren't prepared. It's time for change. Trust this process.

If you follow this program, utilize the resources, do the homework, and commit to applying what you learn, you will walk away with a sense of internal confidence that knows no bounds. You will be in such a stable and grounded place that you will be available for a healthy, loving relationship. The energy you will radiate can only be met by the same level of energy. You will no longer tolerate anything but total respect. You will understand how to communicate and also be heard. You will learn to listen to others and resolve conflict in a way that only allows for a deeper connection.

Now, you are ready to show up, world-class style. You are also saying *Enough is enough.* You are saying *I want to feel confident, empowered, and I want to share my life with someone who will respect, cherish, and honor me.* You are no longer looking for power outside of yourself; you are going within, digging deep, and drawing out the power that already exists inside of you.

To recap, complete the Grid. Decide what your happiness looks like. Then, choose one, maybe two areas to focus on. Please don't take all nine areas of the grid on at once. It will be too overwhelming. While I encourage you to put 100 percent of your energy into this, taking on too much at once will deplete your focus. Choose one or two areas, set a couple short-term, realistic goals. Then, apply this to what you want in your romantic relationship. Create the vision so you have an idea of what you are aiming to accomplish.

Next, set up your daily routine and focus on the three areas: Brain, Biology, and Balance. Track how you access these areas every day. Respect and take care of yourself, and you will begin to respect and care for your entire journey.

Lastly, complete the assessment with the questions I provided. Write your experiences in your journal and watch how you flourish from the inside out.

CHAPTER 2:
How Family Dynamics Affect Your Life Choices

WE ALL COME FROM different backgrounds and styles of families. Whether you were raised in a home with both parents present, lived primarily with one parent, shared equal time in two homes, had a blended family, or were raised by caregivers other than your biological parents, the concept of Family Roles applies to you. This is your family of origin—the people who raised you. Here you will learn about the five Family Roles: Hero, Mascot, Enabler, Scapegoat, and Lost Child.

My family was traditional, in that I grew up with my biological mother, father, and brother. In my family of origin, I have to say I settled into the Enabler Role: I was the "fixer," the one who wanted everyone to be happy. I was the caretaker who people would come to when they were sad or overwhelmed, and I was the one who would help. We were very loving, and I did not experience any major trauma within the family structure as a child. However, when I was at the end of my teenage years, my parents got divorced, which was a complete shocker to me. At that time, I became the mediator, the emotional rock and support for my dad and my mom, passing messages back and forth and holding secrets when I was asked to.

I took on many characteristics of the Enabler, care-taking and dependent, but also as the Hero, being the good child who felt responsible for keeping everything together and looking perfect from the outside. The more I self-reflected, I realized that I even took this to another level and rebelled against the Hero and became a little Scapegoatish. I took advantage of my parents being wrapped up in their divorce and brokenness, and as a senior in high school, I skipped classes, partied, and made the typical bad decisions an unsupervised teen might make. This was the age of learning about boundaries, and without consistency at home, I was teaching myself the concept, quite poorly in fact.

Over the next handful of years, I grew to believe that relationships would complete me as a person. I never questioned if this was right or wrong; it was what I believed in my heart. I cared way too much about what people thought about me and, as my Enabler/ Hero roles indicated, my deepest desire was to be needed as well as take care of others. However, the more I tried to "fix" and fit into the lives of the guys I was attracted to, the more rejection I felt. Confidence tanked, and I just kept repeating the cycle—feeling desperate to be wanted by people who were incapable of a relationship, trying to fix them, failing miserably, personalizing it, and feeling rejected. Wash, rinse, repeat.

You are no doubt already aware of the definition of crazy: repeating the same behavior and hoping for a different outcome? Yes, that's what I did well into my adult years. In my romantic relationships, I developed a pattern where I would dive into a relationship, falling and loving hard. My desires to be accepted and needed probably freaked out a lot of guys because I was ready to settle in and say the big L word after a couple of dates. These men distanced themselves, and each time that happened, I felt emotionally wrecked. Only when I was in my late thirties did I figure out what role I wanted to play in the loving relationships I created. After doing a lot, and I mean *a lot*, of inner work, I now have a much stronger sense of self. I finally feel whole and solid where I stand. I can identify healthy roles in other people, and I have chosen and created a romantic relationship where both my partner and I can relate in a safe and stable way.

As you see, it is common to identify with more than one role. The roles we play may change based on the situation, level of chaos, and ability to manage our situation in times of conflict. By learning about each role, you will relate to some more than others and in doing so, you are creating awareness as to what is healthy and provides positive outcomes in times of stress, and what you do that is unhealthy and results in unhealthy relationships with others as well as yourself.

In this chapter, we'll delve into questions like these: "Why am I attracted to a certain person?" "Why do I seek out partners who aren't healthy for me?" "What makes me behave differently around certain people?" Here's what you can expect to learn and apply to your specific situation:

- Learn how your family of origin influenced the role you gravitate toward

- Define each Family Role

- Explore the Family Roles each person played in your family of origin

- Examine how your experiences impact your current relationship choices

- Identify actionable steps to restructure what may be holding you back to find peace and fulfillment in your personal life, as well as within the relationships around you

This chapter is information-packed, so take it slowly and feel free to take breaks to really process the details. By doing so, you can reflect and make the experience personal to your specific situation. A common response from my clients when they first read this chapter is, "I don't really relate with any of these roles," but as we talk further and look at how my clients respond to conflict, they are able to put the puzzle pieces together. Here we go.

YOUR ROLE, YOUR REALITY

Were you the problem-solver everyone else relied on? Maybe you disappeared to avoid conflict. Perhaps you just wanted everyone to get along and did what you could to keep the peace. The role or combination of roles you took on as a child in your family is ingrained in childhood and influences how you interact and connect with others as an adult. This is typically not a role you consciously choose but one you are given and grow into.

During early childhood, you were presented with inevitable life situations, some pleasant and some of conflict. The dynamic of your family of origin, the people who raised you, helped teach or influence how you dealt with that conflict. As a child, you were forced to find ways to react and cope with things when they didn't make sense or were hurtful. When you fell and lightly bumped your head, people either over-exaggerated the situation, offered comfort and encouraged you to get back up and continue to play, yelled at you for being so clumsy, or ignored you. Any of these responses had an impact on your ability to learn to deal with a problematic situation.

You may be familiar with the concepts of Nature vs. Nurture? Nature is the idea that you were born with a predisposition to certain Personality Types, ways of dealing with situations, and the genetics of your biological parents. Nurture refers to the environment in which you were brought up and that influenced your personality and the way you respond to situations. Both nature and nurture influence who you become as an adult. Nature is the framework with which you came into this world, and nurture is the drywall, paint, and accessories you acquire as you get older. Here we will discuss if these accessories are an asset or a hindrance to your framework as well as how to create a structure setting you up for a solid relationship with yourself.

FAMILY OF ORIGIN

The family of origin is the person or collection of people who had the most influence in raising you, starting when you were very young or just born until you left home as a teenager. It may be your biological mother and/or father, but the family of origin could also be a relative, a neighbor, or an adoptive mother or father. The family of origin is extremely significant because they taught you how to trust. They were responsible for taking care of your basic needs—not only food, clothing, and shelter, but also love, touch, and affection. When these basic needs were met consistently, you were taught to trust others and the environment around you. However, when these basic needs were not met, or there were long periods of time during which these needs were not fulfilled, you were taught to distrust others and perhaps to solely rely on yourself or find other ways to get your needs met.

Someone in your family of origin might fail to meet these needs because of addiction; personality disorders; mental illness; monetary, time, or emotional constraints; or other reasons. Whatever the case, the need was not met, and because you were a child or infant, you may have been left to your own devices to get your needs met.

The fact that you are reading this indicates you are ready to take the steps to feel more empowered. You are ready to uncover specific aspects of childhood that influence you to continue to choose a partner who is not beneficial for you. You are also ready to discontinue behaviors that have become destructive and leave you feeling lonely and dissatisfied.

Did you ever repeat a task over and over only to find out later that you were doing it wrong? It did not feel wrong at the time because it made sense and felt okay. You became comfortable doing the task incorrectly, not realizing it was a mistake. When someone brought it to your attention and reprimanded you, self-awareness kicked in, and you learned and subsequently changed your ways. In short, if you do not stop and reflect and analyze your behavior and your choices or pause long enough to hear other people offering you constructive criticism, it is too easy to get comfortable making mistakes. Remember, comfortable does not always mean healthy. So, take the time and really analyze the way you grew up and the role you settled into, and look at this with a critical eye to identify what worked and what did not work as you move forward in your life.

Have you ever noticed that you are attracted to a similar style of person? This does not just happen out of sheer luck. Think about this. You are not attracted to every person who crosses your path, but you've likely had those moments when you locked eyes with someone and felt an instant connection. It was as if you knew them at some point in time. But an instant connection is not always a healthy connection. Why does this connection occur? How do you know whether to act on this impulse or if a more mindful approach is better?

Understanding human behavior and self-improvement is a never-ending process. Questions like these come with gaining insight and being willing to look yourself in the mirror and have an honest conversation. As you read about Family Roles, here is an opportunity to learn what role or roles in other people you are attracted to so you can intently have a healthy, stable relationship.

MODULE 2-
FAMILY GRID

FAMILY ROLE	Strength	Weakness	ATTRACTED TO	Strength	Weakness
Hero			Hero Mascot Lost Child		
Mascot			Hero Lost Child		
Enabler			Enabler Hero		
Scapegoat			Scapegoat Enabler Lost Child		
Lost Child			No one		

The five Family Roles are listed in this diagram. The left-hand side shows the different roles that people may develop in childhood. The right-hand side indicates which roles are attracted to each other as an adult. Use the spaces provided or your journal to take notes about the strengths and weaknesses of each role. You will soon understand how all of this determines who you are attracted to as an adult and what shifts need to be made to have a healthy, loving relationship.

Each Family Role has positive and negative characteristics. However, these roles were developed as a basic form of survival to manage emotion and conflict. Understanding why you developed into a role is where your power to change what no longer serves you comes into play. As you identify with a particular role, a first reaction may be, "What is wrong with me?" Don't worry. You'll soon be able to evaluate and work through ways to strengthen how you react to conflict.

Each role uses specific defense mechanisms as a way of self-protection. A defense mechanism is a method to guard against something that could cause you pain or harm. It is usually an involuntary reaction, something you don't even consciously plan; your body and brain take over as a way to keep you safe. For example, if someone starts yelling at you, you either fight back, run away and hide, or freeze dead in your tracks. These are defense mechanisms when you are presented with a negative situation: fight, flight, or freeze. You can probably think about a variety of situations right now and connect with one of these methods of reaction.

All this talk about roles can be a bit overwhelming, so I'm going to break it down for you and explain it from a different perspective to help it all make sense.

THE FIVE FAMILY ROLES

In order to explain the five Family Roles, I have attached each role to a character in a well-known 1980s movie, *The Breakfast Club*. There are five main characters:

The Jock—Emilio Estevez played Andrew. This will be the Family Hero.

The Nerd—Anthony Michael Hall played Brian. This will be the Mascot.

The Beauty Queen—Molly Ringwald played Claire. This will be the Enabler.

The Rebel—Judd Nelson played Bender. This will be the Scapegoat.

The Recluse—Ally Sheedy played Allison. This will be the Lost Child.

The Family Hero

Emilio Estevez's character, Andrew Clark, depicts the Family Hero perfectly. Andrew is the classic jock, best wrestler in the school, likely to get a full-ride athletic scholarship to college. The external validation Andrew gets from his teachers and his parents for these successes builds his confidence. Being a wrestler is what his father has drilled into his head, communicating that if he's not the best, he is nothing.

Does Andrew even like wrestling? What kind of pressure to be the best, to look the best, is put on him? Everything appears to be perfect in Andrew's life from the outside.

But cracking the exterior shell, we see a different story. Andrew is sad; he fears rejection from his father if he isn't the best, and he avoids exhibiting negative emotions so as not to disappoint other people. Andrew got into detention because his dad encouraged him to be a tough guy and tape another student's butt cheeks together. He didn't want to participate in such a horrific act but felt pressure to make his dad proud of him.

Positive characteristics of the Hero include being responsible, successful, hardworking, and diligent. They aren't afraid to take risks and push the limit. Heroes are charming, and people are very attracted to them. They can have perfectionistic traits, which could be a positive or a negative. If you needed to have brain surgery, you'd want your surgeon to be a complete perfectionist, but could you be married to a complete perfectionist? Likely not.

Some of the negative aspects of the Hero include being narcissistic or self-centered, often in denial of their feelings, having a fear of failure, and seeking others' approval to feel reassurance. Although the Hero may appear to have incredible confidence, these negative aspects are actually compensating for a high level of insecurity. By always being right or only thinking of themselves, they feel protected from vulnerability. By striving to be the most successful, they are afraid of being seen as a failure. Appearing successful is driven by a fear of looking bad rather than a desire for actual success. See the difference? A lot of times, this is demonstrated by power over others instead of a sense of empowerment within.

A defense mechanism the Hero uses when presented with conflict is to disengage from family members who are dysfunctional. Anything that appears to be chaotic in other people makes a Hero uncomfortable, and so they back away, only wanting to participate in what feels strong and powerful. They can seem insensitive to other people's problems because of their own fear of having to look at themselves in the mirror. Another defense mechanism is obsessive-compulsive behavior. This is exhibited by repetitious thoughts and rigid routines, offering a false sense of control. Perfectionism, as discussed earlier, can be a defense mechanism because if the Hero can keep everything perfect, they feel a sense of control. However, this easily backfires and can create anxiety and depression for the Hero.

Can you see Andrew's role as the Family Hero? As the movie progresses, we become aware of his vulnerability: he wishes his dad accepted him for who he is and worries he'll never measure up. He can't communicate this to his dad, so Andrew avoids telling him how he really feels.

Do you relate to the Hero role? Can you identify anyone in your family or anyone you've been in a romantic relationship with who shares these characteristics? Make a note of it, and we will revisit this.

The Mascot

Anthony Michael Hall's character, Brian Johnson, depicts a couple of roles, but primarily the Mascot. He has underlying characteristics of the Hero. Brian received detention because he brought a flare gun to school with the intention to complete suicide. The gun went off in his locker, and he got in trouble.

Brian displays goofy behavior and says goofy things. He's seen putting a pen up his nose and repeating, "Who do

I think I am?" to himself. He uses goofy behaviors to try and get accepted by the popular crowd.

Brian also has characteristics of the Family Hero. He wants to be the good kid in the family. He's a rule follower and wants people to see him in a positive light. Although he doesn't strive to be the center of attention, Brian will do anything to get accepted. Behind the goofy exterior, he eventually expresses the mounting pressure of being rejected and the overwhelming sadness and disconnect in his life that brought him to the decision to kill himself. He also unleashes his pent-up anger, questions the other characters' authenticity, and expresses his disgust of roles and stereotypes.

The Mascot is the goofball in the family. They are usually fun to be around and will turn your frown upside down. The Mascots are positive and funny and help make light of a negative situation. They are the entertainers of the group and like to be the center of attention.

On the negative side, they hide their pain with humor, so the unresolved, negative issues pile up inside. Internally, the Mascot is afraid and highly insecure and often feels inadequate. The Mascot entertains others to distract from a situation that presents with emotional intensity and conflict. As with the Hero, the Mascot's ignored issues go unresolved; instead, they fester and can eventually lead to anxiety and depression. Mascots are known to avoid responsibilities and accountability by wiggling out of obligations and blaming others.

The defense mechanism of the Mascot is diversion. By using humor, they avoid conflict in order to feel safe. Can you see Brian's role as the Mascot? As the movie progresses, we see him become more and more vulnerable until eventually he breaks down and starts crying. All goofiness set aside, he describes the level of rejection he feels and his desire for people to like him. By avoiding talking about it and reaching out for help, he let the emotion mount to the point where he wanted to die.

Do you or others in your family relate to the Mascot? Are you drawn to the Mascot in romantic relationships? Please note this for further reference.

The Enabler

Molly Ringwald's character, Claire Standish, depicts the Enabler, with a little Family Hero mixed in. Claire is the popular prom queen ideal. Everyone likes Claire. She dresses in all the latest fashion and hangs out with all the cool people. She also comes from a wealthy family where outward appearances matter most.

Claire received detention because she gave into peer pressure, skipped classes, and went shopping with her friends. Her Hero characteristic is to appear perfect from the outside. Internally, she lacks confidence. By people-pleasing, she has lost her internal sense of self. All she wants is for her arguing parents to get along. Claire relies on external factors to feel accepted and will morph herself into what she thinks other people want her to be.

The Enabler is the softest, warmest, fluffiest teddy bear who is wonderful to hug and snuggle with as they offer comfort and acceptance. They're intuitive and acutely aware of people around them. By being aware of others, they know how to act in specific situations to be accepted. They are emotionally involved deeply in people's lives, sometimes to a fault. The Enabler is easy to trust, and because they build relationships easily, they also are the secret holders.

Some of the negative traits of the Enabler include the tendency to form addictions, desperately seeking anything to fill the void of the loss of self. The Enabler relies on people's approval, so they can use manipulation as a form of connection. Crisis is a common theme in the Enabler's life, so if it doesn't exist, they are masters at creating it. There is usually a high level of drama in their lives. This allows them to be the center of attention. They learn that if there is a crisis, people will show affection, which helps them feel wanted and cared for.

A defense mechanism for Enablers is justification and rationalization—two ways to avoid holding people responsible for negative behavior such as addiction. By making other family members feel okay for their bad choices, the Enabler creates a "close" relationship but avoids the conflict, leaving unresolved issues.

Can you relate as the people-pleasing type? Do you compromise yourself to make other people happy? Are you attracted to characteristics in a relationship? Write it down and hang tight.

The Scapegoat

Normally when we hear the word "Scapegoat," we think of someone who is a victim. Someone who is receiving blame from others. In all actuality, there is truth to this when it comes to Family Roles. The "Scapegoat," as referenced in the Family Role dynamic, has been victimized. As you read, you'll note all of the insecurities the Scapegoat holds so far under the surface. Instead of allowing these insecurities to take them down, they become rebellious and go out of their way to not follow rules, defying authority figures. Here is how we'll define the Scapegoat.

Judd Nelson's role, John Bender, perfectly depicts the Scapegoat. He gets detention for falsely pulling the fire alarm and for fighting with teachers and students. Bender comes from an abusive family and instead of dealing with his trauma, he reflects abusive behavior onto other people. He bullies Brian and Andrew and sexually harasses Claire. Bender is a punk and wants to rebel against social standards and rules. He appears tough on the exterior, trusting no one. He sabotages experiences that may have a positive outcome for fear of actually enjoying something and having it ripped away.

The Scapegoat is a very independent-minded person who questions authority to develop their own opinions. They stand strong in these opinions and are not easily manipulated by other family members. Scapegoats are the leaders of a protest, proudly fighting for what they believe in. Sometimes they may join a protest just to rebel against something and outwardly express their opinion.

The downside? Positivity in life is terrifying to the Scapegoat because they own a mindset of "Nothing good lasts forever." The fear of loss causes the Scapegoat to sabotage an event or emotion that is going well. This gives them a sense of control because now the focus is about hurting others before they get hurt. It is the motto of being prepared, but instead of avoiding mistakes and accidents, the Scapegoat creates chaos and damages relationships to avoid deep connections. Internally, the Scapegoat feels hurt, rejection, and shame. They internalize the family's dysfunction and blame themselves.

The defense mechanism for the Scapegoat is projection. They project their hurt, rejection, and shame onto other people. They blame others for making them feel so horrible.

The Scapegoat is the black sheep of the family and is labeled as problematic. However, this defiant behavior can be caused by the family's dysfunction. If there is the Scapegoat to blame, the family issues are avoided.

Can you identify aspects of the Scapegoat in John Bender? We see his vulnerability as he masks his own sadness by overcompensating for it with anger. He really wants to connect with Claire, but fearing rejection, he is cruel to her. He wants to be accepted and feel a part of a group, a relationship, but his angry exterior creates such a boundary that no one can penetrate it to get close.

Do you have some rebel in you? Are you attracted to the "bad boy" type? Take note. We'll be right back to that.

The Lost Child

Ally Sheedy's character, Allison Reynolds, is the typical Lost Child. She is the "weird" recluse who gets into detention, well, because she was bored and wanted something to do. She doesn't fit into any social circles and pushes away anyone who wants to get to know her by either dismissing their efforts or by her bizarre behavior. We see Allison scratching her head over the table and watching flakes fall onto it, which disgusts the other characters, making them want to distance themselves from her.

The Lost Child is out there in the cold, lonely, wandering from town to town, warming their toes momentarily before packing up and moving on. The direction is nowhere, and the connections are lost. Wishing for a sense of belonging but so detached from emotion that those embodying this role find it impossible to bridge the gap with others.

They keep to themselves, do not require much attention, and lead a simple life. They are independent and slide under the radar in dysfunctional families. They can be deadened to emotions and appear apathetic.

The Lost Child sees the family dysfunction clearly but steps away from it. They have watched siblings get in trouble from afar. They are secretive about their lives for fear of being judged. At times, they sabotage their successes out of not feeling deserving. Requiring a drama-free life, they maintain control over the amount of extreme emotion they allow into their existence. Each day may be relatively predictable, which offers a stability the Lost Child can settle into.

The defense mechanism of the Lost Child is retreat. By stepping away and not looking back, they can avoid chaos.

Do you see Allison's role as Lost Child? As the movie progresses, we witness her vulnerability when she acknowledges the dysfunction in her home life and admits to feeling sad and disconnected. One of Allison's memorable lines is, "When you grow up, your heart dies," which demonstrates the deadened emotions of the Lost Child.

Do you have tendencies of the Lost Child, just wanting to defect from your family, trying to understand how you got mixed up in that group in the first place? Are you attracted to someone who is incapable of showing love and affection? Jot it down.

These are the Family Roles.

You may identify with one or a combination of a couple. As an adult, you may see yourself playing one role in a work setting but another role in your relationship. When you are confident, you may play one role, but when you feel insecure, you may play another one. As a child, you may have gravitated toward one role, but as an adult, you may have shifted to a different one.

WHO'S ATTRACTED TO WHOM?

Now, we're going to look at which roles are attracted to each other, why, and what unhealthy patterns could develop if they lack awareness of their intention. Did you take a few notes on this earlier? I hope so.

Family Hero

The Family Hero is likely attracted to another Family Hero. This may look like the perfect pair, two powerhouse, successful people. All looks great on the surface, no problems, but also no depth. Both likely have unresolved issues, which they continue to avoid. There doesn't appear to be conflict, but what relationship doesn't have conflict? Probably the one where conflict is avoided. Over time, issues that are swept under the rug with no resolution will result in resentment, and resentment will quickly kill a relationship.

The Family Hero is also attracted to the Mascot. Again, this is a surface relationship where it looks fun, playful, and carefree. However, it can lack intimacy because of the avoidance of conflict and emotion.

The Family Hero may also be attracted to the Lost Child because they are both void of expressing deeper feelings and avoid connecting with others on an intimate level. But because the Hero thrives on attention, they feel unfulfilled because the Lost Child does not need anyone and has zero desire to dote on the Hero.

Mascot

The Mascot is often attracted to the Family Hero, whom they think can save them from the underlying negative and fearful emotions they hide. The outcome is a shallow relationship with unresolved feelings that can fester and deteriorate their confidence.

The Mascot may also be attracted to the Lost Child because the Mascot can relate to hiding depression with avoidance.

Enabler

The Enabler is attracted to the Family Hero because they present with confidence and charm. Because the Hero is emotionally unavailable and insensitive to others, the Enabler is unfulfilled.

The Enabler is also attracted to another Enabler, but this can be a very co-dependent and enmeshed relationship. Wanting to make each other happy at the cost of their own happiness, they risk the loss of a sense of self and diminished confidence.

Scapegoat

The Scapegoat is attracted to another Scapegoat because they are partners in crime.

The Scapegoat is also attracted to the Lost Child, whose emotions are deadened. However, the Lost Child can be a victim of manipulation and bully behavior.

The Scapegoat can also be attracted to the Enabler as a sense of power and control. The Enabler will allow a Scapegoat to create havoc, and then the Enabler will make excuses and justify the Scapegoat's behavior. The Enabler is an easy target for being manipulated, and this relationship risks having abusive qualities.

Lost Child

The Lost Child is a loner and is not attracted to anyone. They prefer to be reclusive and isolated. Here is where they feel safe. Is it healthy?

If you were able to identify the types of people you are attracted to, use the information above to see where the relationship may have dysfunctional aspects. Are you or were you fulfilled in these relationships? What was missing? Use the chart to fill in what resonates with your specific situation. Use your journal to elaborate on the insights you gain.

RECOMMENDATIONS FOR SELF-IMPROVEMENT WITH EACH ROLE

As stated, each Family Role has strengths and weaknesses. Have you identified aspects of yourself in a few roles so far? If so, it is likely you are focusing on the negative aspects and may feel a heaviness in your body. This is an opportunity for growth. The experiences you have been through have shaped you into who you are today, the good and the bad. However, this doesn't mean that who you are today is who you have to be tomorrow. Each day presents a chance to make small or large shifts toward who you want to be. On the flip side, if you identify aspects of these roles in another person, such as a significant other, friend, colleague, or neighbor, please remember you can't change other people. They must recognize they have an issue and then be willing to make their own changes.

Change in anyone takes time. It's taken you, or them, this much time to ingrain these habits and behaviors; it is going to take some time to recreate healthy patterns. Patience and hard work are your companions during this process.

The ability to gain insight and awareness into your own behavior is the first step to being able to change what may be creating loneliness and disconnect in your life. Here we will discuss opportunities that each role requires to strengthen themselves. Can you identify a common theme?

Hero

Even though the hero appears to have the world in their hands, insecurities lurk under the surface. Questioning themselves and relying on internal factors instead of external gratification causes fear and uncertainty. Taking a look in the mirror, the Hero must acknowledge their faults, their weaknesses, and this can be terrifying because they sense a loss of control over their lives. Feeling vulnerable is scary and sometimes overwhelming to them. The Hero needs to learn to rely on their internal sense of self by slowing down to actually feel their emotions, reflecting on their behavior, and then stopping to evaluate how others are experiencing them.

Without conscious awareness, a Hero could be like a person driving in a car. As they cruise down the road of life, they peer out in front of them and see the world as their stage. They pass manicured lawns, white picket fences, gorgeous, lush gardens, happy smiling faces waving to them in all their glory. However, if they glance in the rear-view mirror, they may find that they have plowed over mailboxes, dug tire tracks through the green lawns, knocked over the people who are no longer smiling but instead licking their wounds. Unaware of the damage they have caused to other people, they continue on their merry way. Does this promote healthy connections with others? Of course not. The Hero must become comfortable with slowing down and checking in with other people. Maybe even asking others what their perceptions of them are and actually listening.

The next step for the Hero is identifying areas of emotion that they avoid, understanding what feelings of fear are lurking just under the surface and learning to work through the discomfort. They may need to pay attention to their internal dialogue, how they speak to themselves. The Hero must allow grace by cutting themselves some slack, allowing mistakes to be made, and learning to embrace what is uncomfortable.

Mascot

Everyone loves the fun guy or gal, but when the Mascot has glimpses of an emotion other than laughter, the realization of loneliness is a stab in the heart.

Many famous comedians carry the Family Role of Mascot. Many famous comedians suffer from major depression, too, and some succumb to suicide as a result.

When people experience trauma in their lives, they are required to utilize coping mechanisms to manage the fear and anxiety. Without healthy coping skills, these feelings are avoided, and the Mascot uses humor to mask the underlying emotion. It doesn't mean the trauma goes away or is forgotten, but the Mascot becomes a professional at burying these feelings in hopes of never having to experience the pain associated with trauma.

In the hustle and bustle of laughing through life, the Mascot avoids personal responsibility and accountability. What would it look like to be in a relationship with a Mascot? If it isn't their fault, whose is it? Owning their actions allows a Mascot to come back to reality with the rest of us, and it creates a connection deeper than surface-level. However, owning feelings of regret, fear, and sadness can be retraumatizing to the Mascot, which may lead to more avoidance.

Accessing professional counseling can help the Mascot begin the process of connecting internally and safely working toward finding peace without being "on stage." The hope is that they take advantage of the assistance from counseling, podcasts, and books to gain a stronger sense of self and learn healthy coping mechanisms when needed.

Enabler

With the intense desire to be accepted, accompanied by fear of letting go and being unneeded, the Enabler utilizes people-pleasing behaviors to connect. A chameleon who changes its colors a hundred times in a day can begin to think it could be a lion instead. Likewise, the Enabler is likely to morph into what other people want them to be and risks completely losing who they really are. The Enabler must learn to form healthy boundaries: *here is where I start and where I end*. By understanding the meaning of "Stay in your lane," the Enabler will learn to respect themselves and those around them.

One method used to develop boundaries is to pause and connect a feeling to a situation. Practicing this several times a day and asking themselves, *How do I feel? What do I want?* while learning to develop a stronger sense of self can become a new habit. The Enabler must learn to be assertive and not rely on passive-aggressive behavior to get their intentions across. Passive-aggressive behavior will likely fail, resulting in rejection and lower self-confidence. The Enabler must also be aware of their inner dialogue and offer empowering statements to themselves.

Defining the differences between having a sense of control and being controlling over other people is an important task for the Enabler. We will delve into this as we continue our journey through the jungle.

By finding stability within, the Enabler will be able to create healthy relationships with people around them. The Enabler will then be able to draw people toward them because others want to be there, not because they feel they have to.

Scapegoat

Oh, the Scapegoat wears many hats, screaming words of "I don't care about anything," "I'm the badass," and "Conformity is for losers." However, the hats a Scapegoat wishes they could wear scream words of "Please accept me," "I wish I felt safe in the world," and "Vulnerability scares me, but I wish I could feel it." It's sad to know that fear of connecting creates such havoc in a Scapegoat's life.

The Scapegoat will benefit from learning to trust themselves to make good decisions and learning to trust that when life is going well, it's okay to enjoy it. As noted earlier, they are likely to throw a monkey wrench into positivity for fear the negativity is inevitable. Therefore, the Scapegoat must pause and understand why they won't allow themselves to be vulnerable. They must ask themselves what they are afraid of in experiencing that level of exposure. Again, professional help from a counselor is most advised because when you start removing the layers of protection, things that have been tucked away in dark corners peek out and can be anxiety-provoking.

It is easier to be angry with claws protracted than it is to feel scared and unprotected. The Scapegoat must develop healthy coping mechanisms to learn to deal with the raw emotion that lies behind those claws. When they practice expressing this level of behavior and cognitive thought process while also applying the coping skills to deal with conflict, confidence grows and the layers of armor fall to the floor.

Lost Child

Isolation and detachment aren't always unhealthy, but too much of a good thing turns into not such a great thing. Introverted people find solace in their alone time, but the Lost Child is isolating as a coping mechanism to avoid negative emotions. Therefore, the intention behind the reclusive behavior is not healthy, and the confidence will diminish over time. Although they might feel in control of the castle walls they have built to keep people out, the inside can get cold and lonely after a time.

The Lost Child must pause and learn to identify why they are drawn to this role. They must ask themselves what they are avoiding. Is it the inability to deal with conflict? Was it easier to slink off to the side when chaos ensued? Developing coping mechanisms to put into place when negativity occurs will help the Lost Child face some of their own hidden traumas. Learning to slightly trust the world will help them lower the drawbridge and begin to practice connecting with others. They may never become the center of attention, but working away from the extreme of complete isolation could bring confidence and a stronger sense of self to the Lost Child.

Fear of rejection keeps the Lost Child from taking the risk to connect with others. Even when someone shows them an authentic sense of friendship or love, the Lost Child does not trust it to be true and may sabotage it. Learning to be assertive will help the Lost Child confront what is scary and know they have the confidence to manage the emotions in a healthy way.

COPING STATEMENTS

Almost twenty years ago, my colleague and mentor, Barbara Basile, taught me about something called a coping statement. A coping statement is a mantra that you repeat to yourself one hundred times a day for two weeks straight. It is something that you do not believe at the time, but as you ingrain the statement into your brain, you begin to believe it.

You probably already do this, but with negative statements such as, "No one will ever love me." Over time, you don't leave room in your mind for the positive alternative and can subconsciously create the reality that no one will ever love you.

The one I chose was, "I don't need to prove myself to anyone." I melted it into my mind, and today, when I am in a situation where I am losing my sense of self or worrying too much about what others think, the statement pops into my head and offers a moment of pause and reflection.

Here are examples of possible coping statements for each Family Role:

Hero

"My partner's needs are as important as mine."

Mascot

"It is safe to ask myself how I truly feel."

Enabler

"I respect myself and deserve respect from others."

Scapegoat

"I can let my guard down and learn to trust."

Lost Child

"I am worthy of love."

The goal here is to take the judgment out of the perception of each role and look at them for what they are. They are groupings. They are not good, bad, right, or wrong. They just are. The power comes in identifying what role you gravitate toward and understanding what challenges present themselves in terms of creating and maintaining healthy relationships, not just with other people but with yourself.

By looking at how the role or roles influenced you to where you are today, you can evaluate areas of gains and setbacks in your life. By analyzing aspects that work or areas that just aren't working in your favor, you will now have the opportunity to change. Also, by identifying the types of roles you are attracted to, you may gain knowledge of why some relationships are more challenging or why you frequently feel so empty. You may also understand why some relationships are easy and make you feel like you can completely be yourself. Learning this skill set will allow you not only to be your best self but to create healthy relationships with others.

Take some time to identify what role you developed into as a child and how that has played out in your adulthood. Answer the questions and examine these roles and determine what you might change moving forward. What is helping you feel confident, have a sense of control over your life, and avoid feeling dependent on others? Are these areas of concern for you? Why? What role would you like to shift into?

SELF-REFLECTION

Journal prompt: Family Roles

In your journal, take some time and thoughtfully answer these questions. Feel free to elaborate. The more you write, the more personal you will make your experience.

- What's my previous and current Family Role?

- What worked and didn't work?

- What do I want my role to be in a significant partner relationship?

- What do I want a partner's role to be?

CHAPTER 3:
Attachment Styles and Personality Types

WHEN I AM WORKING with clients in my private practice, I encourage them to understand the *why* behind the behavior instead of only the behavior itself. If you just react to what you initially see, I guarantee that you're missing the gold mine. Say your car just stopped running one day. Wouldn't you wonder why? You wouldn't just start beating on your car. Well, maybe you would, but eventually, you would wonder, **What happened? What made my car stop running**? Here, you will learn where behaviors come from and why we react when we are faced with conflict or with fear.

In this chapter, you will identify which of the four Attachment Styles you experienced as a child: Secure, Anxious, Avoidant, and Fearful. Then, you will understand how that style, while influenced by your life experiences, developed your Personality Type. Stable, Dependent, Antisocial, Narcissistic, and Borderline. By putting this all together, you will have the opportunity to change what may be holding you back from experiencing a confident, secure relationship as an adult.

The following quotes demonstrate attitudes toward romantic relationships, and each quote is connected to an Attachment Style.

"Hey, let's hang out and get to know each other!"

"I need you!"

"Leave me alone!"

"I need you, but go away!"

Have you ever said anything like these? Have you heard them from a partner? Understanding the *why* behind these statements will shed light on the layers covering the true rooted behavior. There is your goldmine I spoke of.

Attachment theory, which goes all the way back to 1950, was developed by John Bowlby, who studied how infants reacted when they were separated from their primary caregivers. Then he studied how they reacted when they were presented with a conflict or startling experience, and finally, how the infant reacted when they were reunited with their caregivers. He studied the demeanor of each caregiver and what effect that had on the infant's ability to cope with conflict. Further, he theorized that humans need other humans to survive; however, if there were inconsistencies in the caregiving an infant or toddler experienced, the child's level of trust in others was compromised. Inconsistencies are defined as not attending to the basic needs of a baby ages zero to three, which include feeding, clothing, sheltering, and loving.

Mary Ainsworth came along in 1970 and defined the different types of attachment and further added that the way a baby experiences attachment defines its ability to trust people and the world around it.

Think of it this way. If a person were alone in the prehistoric days, they would likely get eaten or die somehow by not being protected. An infant is 100 percent dependent on its caregiver for protection and basic needs. If those needs are consistent, the infant learns to trust the world around it. If those needs are inconsistent, it learns to survive any way it possibly can, using manipulation, avoidance, or hypersensitivity. While that makes sense from a survival standpoint, if you are in a relationship and you lack the ability to trust your partner securely and confidently, the relationship can become dysfunctional.

I've always found attachment theory fascinating because it so clearly depicts why people behave, think, and feel the way they do. As with anything, there is a spectrum of what inconsistency means. The level of trauma, abuse, and/or neglect a baby experiences from birth to age three directly correlates to their level of non-attachment as well as the level of dysfunction in their personality.

Before you go blaming your parents for everything or beating yourself up because you forgot to pick up your baby from daycare (yep, I did it too), calm down a bit. No matter what, we've all experienced inconsistencies while growing up or while raising our little ones because we are humans, and humans are imperfect! Because of these experiences, we are all a little neurotic. I remember sometime before the age of three, I got separated from my parents at the grocery store. Somewhere in my little mind, I thought it was a good idea to go into the parking lot to see if the car were there, as if I'd recognize the car. Still, I made it back into the store and found my dad's leg, which I always hugged. Imagine the additional trauma when I looked up and the person whose leg I was hugging wasn't my dad! Forty-six years later, I still tease my parents for creating this hot mess.

The goal here is to understand the brass tacks that give us the power to grow, become stronger, and gain control over aspects we had no idea about. This will all make better sense soon, so stick with me!

Trust, empathy, and vulnerability are major players when it comes to creating healthy, intimate relationships. *Woah*, you say. When I bring up these words to my more guarded clients, I see them shift in their seats and reach for their water bottles. Yeah, these are powerful words that elicit some deep emotion, but the ability to demonstrate these three words is crucial to have a healthy relationship with yourself and with those around you. These three concepts are established during the attachment phase, all the way back to before the age of three.

Between birth and three years of age, we learn how to trust, be vulnerable, and develop empathy. The ability to learn these three essential aspects as a young child will set the course for how we create and maintain close, loving relationships for the rest of our lives. Imagine what a crucial time this is and how important the ability to trust, be vulnerable, and empathize with others is throughout your life.

During this early stage of life, we have only basic needs: food, clothing, shelter, and love. However basic these needs are, we would die if they were not provided. Not only is it crucial that we have these survival staples, but they must be met with consistency. If a baby goes hungry for hours, sits in dirty diapers, has a wild schedule, or is hardly held and loved, that baby must learn to survive and cope with such anxiety and uncertainty. These coping skills influence how the baby develops a sense of trust in other people and its environment.

Some automatic ways of thinking for this little person include the following:

- Can I count on you to take care of me?

- Can I trust you will show up and follow through with your responsibility?

- If I'm not automatically getting my need met, how must I manipulate the situation so I can survive?

- Am I going to be left to rely only on myself to get my needs met?

- Will you meet my needs and take good care of me?

Lacking the ability to trust people whom we are attempting to build a relationship with creates unhealthy patterns. Behaviors that indicate a lack of trust are jealousy, control, and manipulation, to name a few. Not trusting also results in an inability to be vulnerable. This is demonstrated by shutting down, staying guarded, and not communicating our needs. Being able to trust and be vulnerable allows the baby to learn empathy. Empathy is the ability to share and understand the emotions of another person and have compassion for what other people are dealing with. Without trust and vulnerability, a person is not able to put themselves in another person's shoes. A person's ability to feel and show empathy is directly related to the type of attachment they experienced as a baby.

MODULE 3 - ATTACHMENT STYLES & PERSONALITY TYPES

SECURE

Confident

Not Defensive

Comfortable with Intimacy

"Hang out and stay awhile"

Little to no personality disorder

ANXIOUS

Preoccupied with relationships

Low emotional regulation

Impulsive and reactive

"I need you!"

Dependent Personality

AVOIDANT

Dismissive

Overly positive view of self

Negative view of others

"Leave me alone"

Antisocial Personality Disorder
Narcissistic Personality Disorder

FEARFUL

Afraid of Intimacy

Very low emotional regulation

Fears Rejection

"I need you but go away!"

Borderline Personality Disorder

As you see in this diagram, there are four Attachment Styles. We will talk about both childhood attachment and adult attachment. Childhood attachment is what you experienced from the caregiver from birth to age three. Adult attachment is the influence of what you experienced as a child, combined with the life experiences which led you to the way you attach to others in any relationship as an adult.

One more important aspect is being able to understand what your caregiver was dealing with in their lives while they were also caring for you. This is pretty important. When I speak of a caregiver who didn't adequately take care of an infant, it likely raises your hackles. Remember, there are many factors that negatively affect the caretaker, such as addiction, mental illness, or being a single parent forced to work three jobs to get food on the table.

What you will accomplish in this chapter is the following:

- Define the four types of Attachment Styles

- Explore what Attachment Style you gravitate toward

- Identify what conflict the caregiver was dealing with (maybe even associate a Family Role with this person)

- Connect a Personality Type for each Attachment Style

- Understand what is necessary to be available for a healthy relationship based on aspects of each Attachment Style and Personality Type

I am going to associate a fictitious name with each Attachment Style. Ready to do some dissecting?

SECURE ATTACHMENT

Tom grew up with his mom and aunt as his primary care-givers. His father was never in the picture, but because his mom and aunt worked together to raise Tom, he got his needs met consistently. They were quick to respond when Tom needed a diaper change and were sensitive to his needs when he cried or was sick.

Tom's mom and aunt were able to work as a team, taking turns to meet the needs of a small child. When one was frustrated and exhausted, the other stepped in to help. They were over the moon for Tom, held him and hugged him and kissed his cute chubby cheeks every chance they got. They felt secure in themselves to raise him.

As Tom grew up, he developed a strong sense of self, a confidence that he trusted the people around him until they proved themselves otherwise. Tom relied on himself to get his needs met, wasn't afraid to ask for help or set limits with people who seemed to take advantage of him. Once he started to date, he felt comfortable getting close to his partner. He valued her independence and encouraged her to reach for the stars, never getting jealous or wanting to hold her back for fear she would leave him.

Did Tom have insecurities that crept up? Of course he did; this is real life, after all. But Tom was able to look himself in the mirror with a critical eye and set realistic goals for himself to overcome what life threw at him. Despite the fact that his father wasn't in his life, he worked through these issues and was grateful for the love and trust his mom and aunt provided.

Tom felt grounded and solid in himself, and when the right person came around, she was a bonus in his life versus someone he needed to meet his own needs. Regarding his chill and relaxed attitude in a relationship, Tom's tagline is, "Hang out and stay awhile."

ANXIOUS ATTACHMENT

Michelle grew up with her mom and dad as her primary caregivers. Her father worked a job that required him to travel 80 percent of the year. Her mother, a stay-at-home mom, was responsible for taking care of the house and raising Michelle and her sister, who was two years older.

Michelle's mom put a tremendous amount of pressure on herself to be a super mom. She tried to never let the house get messy, to constantly have all the laundry done and to display a manicured yard. She was somehow president of the local mom's club. She seemed to have a million things on her plate, and to others, she balanced all of it. However, behind closed doors, Michelle's mom was inconsistent in her caregiving. Internally, she suffered from severe anxiety.

By staying busy, her mom felt a sense of control, but her anxiety contributed to her inability to be calm and collected. Michelle would go for hours with a dirty diaper while her mom tried to cope with panic attacks. Michelle would also be left in her crib for hours on end, not knowing when her mom would come get her. When her father was home from his travels, Michelle received a little more consistency, which she thoroughly enjoyed, but once her mom was on her own again, Michelle experienced bouts of neglect. When her mom's anxiety would let up, her mom would feel incredibly guilty and try to go overboard with love and affection. But fighting anxiety was a full-time job, and her ability to provide consistency for her children regularly fell short.

Michelle grew up very reactive to people and situations. She could have a hot temper, and the slightest thing would set her off. Others felt she made mountains out of molehills and had difficulty regulating her emotions. Her reactions to situations were incongruent with what the situation presented. This made her feel even more out of control.

Once Michelle started dating, she lost herself and became dependent on her partner to meet all her needs. If they failed to do so, she personalized it and reacted with neediness, which pushed these men farther away. The cycle would continue, and Michelle became impulsive and possessive in her dating life. She compromised any ounce of self-respect just to try and feel wanted by someone else.

She lacked worth and believed that being with a man was the only way to feel good about herself. Regarding her obsessive and dependent attitude in a relationship, Michelle's tagline is, "I need you; don't ever leave me."

AVOIDANT ATTACHMENT

Scott grew up with his grandfather as his primary caregiver. His biological parents died in a car accident just after he was born. His grandfather, a widower, was a very successful businessman. After experiencing the loss of his wife, Scott's grandfather vowed to never get close to another human being again. Instead of allowing himself to grieve, he poured himself into his job, and his emotions became barbed wires.

This didn't bode well for Scott because he was an infant and required an engaging caregiver to meet his basic needs, including loving hugs and kisses. Instead, Scott was left to cry himself to sleep, which could sometimes take hours. He had to deal with nightmares alone. His grandfather became angry if Scott disturbed his sleep, and he'd yell, curse, and call Scott names. Sometimes his grandfather would even mock him, getting in his face with a whiney tone and say things like, "Oh, what are you going to do, cry?" Scott was fed and clothed, but there was no tenderness displayed. He was a chore to his grandfather and the brunt of his grandfather's jokes to his business buddies.

As Scott grew up in a cold, loveless house, he learned that if he wanted to eat, he'd have to fix his own food. He learned to be self-sufficient at too young an age. He learned that people couldn't be trusted, and vulnerability was a weakness. Scott developed an overly positive sense of himself, felt like he was always right, and had a difficult time maintaining friendships.

As you can imagine, he grew to be an angry man, all alone in his big, cold house. Beneath the surface, he wanted to be in a relationship. Women would come and go in his life, and he blamed each of them for being "idiots," "too sensitive," or just a basic "pain in the ass." His relationships were always short-lived, and the ending was always his partner's fault, never his own.

Regarding his negative view of other people, Scott's tagline and attitude about a relationship says, "Leave me alone."

FEARFUL ATTACHMENT

Angie grew up with her mother as the primary caregiver. Angie's biological dad knows nothing about her. Her mother met him one night at the bar, had sex, and got pregnant. She didn't know his name or anything about him. She ended up having Angie but never tried to locate the dad. Angie's mother always had a boyfriend who usually moved in with her, but the relationship only ever lasted two months, tops. The characters she attracted were usually abusive men with drug and alcohol addictions, which Angie's mom struggled with as well.

When Angie was an infant, her mom got into a relationship with a man who was her cocaine dealer. Because she let him move in, the drugs were free. Her mother was extremely paranoid and would hallucinate, which irritated the boyfriend, even though he supplied the drug causing this. He would become angry and hit Angie's mother, and a few times, he even hit little Angie for crying. If anyone had paid attention to her, it was because she was screaming out. Throughout her childhood, Angie witnessed men abusing her mother.

When a boyfriend left, Angie's mother would try to clean up her act, but in her fuzzy, detoxing mind, she couldn't remember if Angie had bathed, eaten, or napped. Furthermore, when she was high or drunk, she was mean and yelled at Angie. At one time, a live-in boyfriend sexually abused Angie. It wasn't until later in life that Angie realized the trauma she had endured as a baby. The person who she was supposed to trust and feel safe with became the person she feared the most. This resulted in her inability to trust people and their intentions, good or bad.

As Angie grew up, she drew people in with her charm, seeking immediate gratification. But when the fear of rejection and abandonment set in, she'd panic. Even when the relationship was on the healthier side, she did everything to sabotage the relationship, proving her inner dialogue that people can never be trusted.

When Angie started dating, there was tremendous pressure on her boyfriends to meet her needs, even though her needs changed on a dime. They would end up walking on eggshells. One minute the boyfriends were held on a pedestal. They were the best thing that ever came into her life. They could do no wrong. But all it took was one slight, one flavor of criticism, even constructive criticism, and WOOSH, they were flushed down the toilet. Partners of Angie's walked on thin ice, and because of this pull-you-close-push-you-away behavior, her relationships didn't last very long.

Regarding her fearful attitude about a relationship, her tagline is a push/pull and says, "I need you, but go away."

PERSONALITY TYPES AND WHAT YOU CAN DO TO OVERCOME THEM

As we have discussed, your personality is based on both nurture and nature. You are likely born into this world with a framework of a predisposed personality, but the influences you experienced during the attachment phase strongly determine how that framework is filled in.

Referring to the previous diagram, you will see the Personality Types listed within each Attachment Style.

The severity of the trauma, abuse, and neglect a child may endure is directly correlated to the intensity of the personality dysfunction. So, the greater the trauma, the more dysfunctional the Personality Types. Without doing the work on yourself, usually with a professional counselor, the negative personality traits grow stronger as a way of survival and getting your basic needs met. Let's visit our characters to see how this plays out.

Having little to no personality disorder

Tom is our Secure Attachment character. Because he grew up with love and healthy discipline and learned healthy ways to communicate and resolve conflict, he is a well-rounded man. He learned to trust and have empathy and learned that being vulnerable is healthy. Tom chose a partner who reciprocates his healthy personality. When conflict arises, Tom knows that he and his partner will figure it out. Even if he must take a time out, he isn't afraid his partner is going to leave the relationship. Healthy love and an honest connection have already been established so Tom doesn't have to flip into survival mode to feel safe.

One time Tom had to borrow his partner's phone to find directions to a restaurant. When he opened it, he saw several calls going back and forth from his partner to a strange, unknown number. Did he flip out? Well, he did have a reaction of sorts because it caught him off guard, but he didn't lose his cool. He immediately brought it up with his partner and gave her a chance to explain that it was a working relationship with a colleague who was new to her office. Because they have a solid trust as a foundation, he believed her, and they were able to have a peaceful dinner.

This is an example of not jumping to conclusions, identifying a source of conflict, and being able to have a rational conversation. This also shows the ability to trust, let go of the conflict, and enjoy the evening. It takes an internal sense of confidence.

Dependent Personality Resulting from Anxious Attachment

Michelle is our Anxious Attachment character, and as a result, she has developed a Dependent Personality. Because her mother was extremely anxious to the point of panic attacks, Michelle's needs were either overly met by her mom doing everything for her, or not met at all because her mom had a hard enough time just taking care of herself. When Michelle's father was in town, the chances of needs being met consistently increased, but he would soon leave again for work.

Anxiety is both hereditary and a learned behavior. When anxiety is high, you question everything about the way you act, to the choices you make, to the thoughts you entertain. When anxiety is high, your confidence is low. If you grow up with an anxious caregiver, not only do they not trust their own intuition, but they likely don't trust that you can take care of yourself either. Infants, toddlers, children, and adolescents need to know their caregivers believe and have confidence in them. When this belief is compromised, the idea of inadequacy is ingrained into consciousness. Michelle's mom, who was overbearing and overprotective, didn't allow Michelle to make mistakes or take calculated risks. This communicated that Michelle must depend on others to meet her own needs.

Michelle met a man I'll call Joe. They have been together for seven years and live apart. When the relationship is good, it is very good, but when it is bad, the fighting and anxiety are off the charts. Because of the good times together, Michelle and Joe keep coming back to each other to try and make the relationship work. Michelle has become dependent on Joe to reassure her and ease her anxiety. However, when she becomes extremely anxious, she lashes out at Joe. Out of defense, Joe goes for days without talking to her. This sends Michelle into a complete tailspin, causing her to call and text him hundreds of times a day and drive by his house while her anxiety sends her into a panic attack. Emotional triggers of her childhood ignite, and she is reminded that she can't trust herself since her mom didn't allow her wiggle room to make mistakes. She doesn't realize the difference in being INTERdependent on someone, which is relying on them to show up in the relationship; being faithful, reliant, respectful, and working as a team. She is DEpendent on Tom and relies on him for everything. Growing up, she didn't gain the courage to learn self-reliance to meet her own needs or learn self-acceptance when she made a mistake because her mom did everything for her. Michelle lacked the confidence that when things go wrong, you pause and evaluate the situation and then proceed forward with a clear mind. So when trouble strikes in the relationship, Michelle just melts down. Her behavior drives Joe farther and farther away, stressing Michelle out even further. Michelle has reached a point where she relies on Joe to make her feel confident in the relationship. Because he doesn't understand anxiety and is conflict-avoidant, he retreats. This only perpetuates the cycle, and Michelle clings to him even more.

Someone with a Dependent Personality has lost their sense of self. They have a difficult time making the simplest decisions on their own, relying on others to do this for them. They are desperate for love and affection. The Dependent person feels their partner completes and fixes them. It is common that even when a positive situation or partner comes along, the Dependent person sabotages it for fear of it ending, as nothing good lasts forever. Other traits of the Dependent person include being clingy, demanding, easily jealous, and getting upset by the smallest of issues.

Dependent people are passive doormats and easily bullied and are therefore perfect targets for abusive relationships. If they disagree with someone, they are likely to shut down, retreat inward, and stop communicating. But when anxiety builds, it is demonstrated by lashing out, not addressing what is actually going on. The underlying issue of someone with a Dependent Personality is fear of abandonment, so they turn themselves inside out trying to please others, losing themselves in the process.

Antisocial Personality and/or Narcissistic Personality resulting from Avoidant Attachment

Scott is our Avoidant Attachment character, and as a result, has developed a Narcissistic Personality. He grew to learn that he could rely only on himself for emotional stability. He learned that trusting people would only disappoint him, and that by having power over others, he could protect himself from being hurt. He became demanding of the people around him, always needing to feel in control. Secretly, Scott always wanted someone to care for him, but the minute a special someone got close, he pushed them away.

Vulnerability was a scary feeling because he never learned to believe someone could have good intentions to love him. He didn't even know if he could reciprocate such an emotion for fear of eventually being rejected. Scott had a few romantic relationships, but eventually, his partners left him because of his verbally and emotionally abusive behavior. He tended to choose people who were passive and allowed him to control them.

One day, Scott had an argument with his boss, lost his temper, and almost lost his job. Instead, his boss sent him to mandatory counseling. He was showing a pattern of intimidation and bullying behavior to people on his team. If his job were not on the line, he would never have entered therapy. This is typical of people with a Narcissistic Personality: they don't feel they have done anything wrong or that they have any problems. They blame everyone around them for their anger. Therapy is usually short-lived with a narcissist because as soon as a therapist calls them out on their behavior, they get angry and refuse to continue.

But Scott went to therapy. He told the therapist what he thought she wanted to hear. He superficially took ownership of his behavior at work and promised to never lose his temper again. He completed the required number of sessions to keep his job. Scott never opened up to the therapist about his childhood for fear she would judge him. He also didn't see a purpose because what was done was done. If everyone around him would just do what he wanted, there wouldn't be any problems. At least that's what he told himself.

Eventually, Scott met a very sweet and soft-spoken woman who was just so happy to be in his company but displayed signs of a Dependent Personality Type. Scott felt powerful when he was with her because she was dependent on him and would do whatever he wanted. This relationship was unhealthy because she became his figurative punching bag; he could treat her in such a negative way, and she would just keep coming back to him. He tolerated her because she made him feel important, but she lost her sense of self in the process. They stayed together, but it was a loveless, unfulfilling relationship.

I want to take a minute to address the other Personality Type in the Avoidant Attachment Style: Antisocial. Antisocial goes far beyond not wanting to be with people. It is a classified diagnosis, also called a sociopath. This is when a person has no regard for other people and no regard for what is right or wrong. These types are extremely manipulative. What separates Antisocial Personality from Narcissism is that Antisocial Personality people have no empathy, no guilt, or no remorse for their behavior. Whereas Scott's Narcissism is an overcompensation for his deep level of insecurity, he knows the difference between right and wrong and secretly wants to be accepted by people. He cares what others think, but the Narcissistic shield keeps him from having to show this fear.

An Antisocial/Sociopath person is very likely to violate the law, become a criminal, and could be a professional con artist, a serial killer, serial rapist, for example. When Antisocial Personality is developed, the person almost always has experienced a horrific childhood of abuse and trauma at a very young age. The trauma is usually repetitive. Being able to learn empathy happens during these crucial ages and is not something that can be taught later in life. As they grow older, these individuals continue to get into trouble and become more defiant. Continuing down that path results in more severe, problematic behavior. Changes that happen are usually due to the person learning to manage their consequences. If they spent ten years in prison, they likely don't want to go back, so they make changes in their lives to avoid prison. The changes, however, don't typically come from an empathetic stance.

Borderline Personality resulting from Fearful Attachment

Growing up, Angie was terrified of anything related to intimacy—not just sex, but holding hands, sitting close to another person, and especially sharing deep feelings. Angie found it difficult, if not impossible, to regulate her feelings. When she was frustrated, she flew into a rage. When she was confused about something, she hit her head against the wall. When she was overwhelmed with her emotions, she cut on her arms and upper thighs. She liked to show the fresh wounds on her arms because that would draw people to her, which gave her a sense that they cared. But if they came too close, Angie would find any way to get mad at them and push them away.

Angie longed for a relationship. When she found someone to connect with, she placed them on a pedestal, bragging to everyone how they could do no wrong. She would create this perfect ideal in the person she met. But no one is perfect. Her fantasized relationship was a setup for failure. One day, Angie and her current boyfriend got home from a party, where she had drunk a little too much. She stumbled into her bedroom, shrugged her dress off her body, climbed into bed, and passed out. The next evening, during an enjoyable dinner, her boyfriend made a joking comment about her dress being in a crumpled pile on the floor. Angie flew off the handle, yelled at him, called him names, and said he was too demanding. She asked why he was so critical and told him she could never please him. She even slapped his face.

What confused her partner was that after this major reaction to something seemingly harmless, Angie broke down, apologizing and telling him that he deserved better. She cried and said her life wasn't worth living and that she should just end it right then and there. Her partner was confused. He was the one who had endured this emotional, verbal, and physical abuse, but he found himself needing to take care of Angie because she was in such a distraught state of mind. So, he put all his emotions aside and cared for her. The next day, Angie acted as if nothing happened and never even apologized for her behavior. He wondered if he'd imagined the whole thing, but when he saw the red mark on his face, he realized the reality of the situation.

Angie had short-term, intense relationships with several men. She could never form long-term friendships or romantic relationships.

This is typical of people with Borderline Personality. Their intense reactions don't match the situations. They often make their partner feel responsible for actions that don't belong to them. Because they feel so out of control in their own lives, they use manipulation to try and feel a sense of being grounded. In the mind of a borderline person, life is either wonderful or a complete disaster. They live in extremes and can change on a dime. This behavior can be very taxing on their partner. In the beginning, the partner tries to help ease the chaotic emotion, but over time, they just lose confidence in themselves because of the mind twisting that occurs. Eventually, both partners spin out of control, and the relationship is doomed.

WHERE TO GO FROM HERE

It is common for all of us to have a little of all these personality traits. We are all somewhat dependent, self-centered, over-reactive. But when the behavior is repetitive and more intense, it's time to take a look at getting control over yourself. I encourage my clients that I work with to assess aspects of their personality and decide if they are creating problems in their lives—they have an opportunity to correct them. If you don't check yourself, these behaviors will result in a very lonely, unfulfilling life.

To make changes, you must first be aware of the behavior. You can't change something if you don't even see it is a problem. On the flip side, if you find yourself in a relationship with a person continuously exhibiting these dysfunctional behaviors, you cannot change that person. They have to be aware and want to change. This is an important concept not just to read here in this book but to know in your heart. If you are working harder for someone to change, harder than the effort they are putting out for their own changes, you will burn out. Simple as that.

I usually work from a cognitive-behavioral theoretical framework with my clients. This means changing your thinking so that you can change your behavior. I always give my clients something to practice, write about, think about outside of each session. This helps them gain awareness of their behavior, so they can stop it when it happens and put healthier behaviors into place. When they realize what isn't working and actually make the shift, resulting in a positive outcome, their confidence increases. The more control they feel in their lives, the lower the anxiety they experience, and the more empowered they are. This equation will work all day long. They begin to rely on themselves for an internal sense of self instead of depending on external reinforcement. What a difference this makes for them. What a difference it will make for you.

There are ways to improve each Attachment Style and Personality Type based on the symptoms they display. Here is what you will learn in this chapter:

- The specific traits of each type (from the DSM-V 2013 manual)

- Suggestions for each type regarding how to strengthen their sense of self

- How to tell what Personality Type your partner carries

ANXIOUS ATTACHMENT PERSONALITY TYPE: DEPENDENT CHARACTERISTICS LOOK LIKE THIS:

1. Difficulty making routine decisions without input, reassurance, and advice from others

2. Requires others to assume responsibilities that they should be attending to

3. Fear of disagreeing with others and risking disapproval

4. Difficulty starting projects without support from others

5. Excessive need to be nurtured and supported by others, even allowing others to impose themselves and not speak up in opposition rather than speak up and risk rejection or disapproval

6. Feels vulnerable and helpless when alone

7. Desperately seeks another relationship when one ends

8. Unrealistic preoccupation with being left alone and unable to care for themselves (American Psychiatric Association, 2013)

Ways to strengthen the sense of self with Dependent Personality:

People with Dependent Personality are likely to enter therapy voluntarily. They have good insight into their brokenness. They come to me because they are either in very toxic relationships and feel they can't get out, or they have just experienced another failed relationship. The anxiety they feel after being left is so intense that they seek anything to get some relief.

Because anxiety is the presenting issue, I first help clients learn what anxiety is and how to manage their symptoms. When the anxiety is high, the confidence is low, and when the confidence is high, the anxiety is low. Because anxiety is about not having a sense of control over your life, I help them learn to identify what they can control versus what they cannot control. The best and fastest way to improve confidence is to set short-term, realistic goals. They have to be short-term so you get instant gratification, which gives you encouragement to meet your goal, and they have to be realistic so you aren't setting yourself up to fail. I teach the Dependent Personality Type to own their behavior so they can learn to own their feelings. Another area of focus is helping them rely on themselves for internal satisfaction instead of relying solely on other people to make them feel whole and worthy of love. The external gratification is attractive because you instantly feel wonderful, but it is risky because it can go away, and you are left with nothing. However, if you learn to strengthen your internal sense of self, you will have that forever, and no one can ever take it from you.

Helping a Dependent person develop a list of what they want in a relationship or what they want in their lives is important. Oftentimes, they have never even asked themselves these questions because they are constantly meeting the needs of others. So, we create a list of what it would look like in their lives if they were happy and at peace. Creating a list of non-negotiables is just as crucial as committing to the list.

How do you know if your partner is Dependent? The following red flags may be helpful. Dependent Personality Types:

- Are emotionally intense

- Need to be taken of

- Shift blame to their partner and make them feel responsible for all the issues

- Have a victim mentality, feeling like everything bad is always happening to them without the ability to make change in their own lives. This perpetuates the feelings of being out of control

- Are emotionally taxing on their partner

- Have high anxiety and low confidence

- Do not trust themselves to fulfill their own individual needs

AVOIDANT ATTACHMENT PERSONALITY TYPES: NARCISSISTIC/ANTISOCIAL/SOCIOPATH CHARACTER-ISTICS LOOK LIKE THIS:

1. Grandiosity with expectations of superior, best of the best, top-shelf type treatment from other people

2. Fixated on fantasies of power, success, intelligence, attractiveness, etc.

3. Self-perception of being unique, superior, and associated with high-status people and institutions

4. Need continual admiration from others

5. Sense of entitlement to special treatment and to obedience from others

6. Exploitative of others to achieve personal gain

7. Unwilling to empathize with the feelings, wishes, and needs of other people

8. Intensely envious of others, and the belief that others are equally envious of them

9. Pompous and arrogant demeanor (American Psychiatric Association, 2013)

Ways to strengthen the sense of self with Narcissistic/ Antisocial/ Sociopath Personality:

Many theorists say you cannot teach empathy. If it is not developed before age three, the window of opportunity is missed. It took me years in my professional career to admit that this is true.

My first job within the mental health world was as a counselor at a juvenile hall in Southern California. Fresh out of college, optimistic as hell, I remember calling my mom when I was offered the job and telling her I was at the library to learn about gangs. "Um, what?" she asked. Was I in for a shocker?! But I worked there for five years and learned about criminal behavior, family dynamics, and what a lack of empathy looked like. I got to know the kids because they would frequently come in and out of the system. As nice as they were to me during groups and physical education, they'd just as soon throw me to the ground, take my keys, and escape without a blink of an eye. The inability to connect for some of these kids was heartbreaking, but as I learned their stories of unimaginable abuse and neglect, I understood why they would likely never trust a soul. I would be so sad to think of what a kid, at the age of sixteen, was in store for.

A decade later, I conducted court-ordered groups for perpetrators of domestic violence. I had a men's group and a women's group. Every now and then, a member would pass through, and I'd get chills on my neck as I realized their eyes seemed hollow and the empathy was non-existent. The lack of care for another person is quite astonishing. They would complete their thirty-six weeks of groups, but even on graduation day, there was nothing. They'd either be back with me or in jail at some point. Teaching them consequence management was the best I could do for them.

Now, in my private practice, I rarely have Narcissists or Antisocial type clients. Although I do work with people exhibiting this behavior, they don't often enter therapy voluntarily. If they do come, it is usually because their spouse gave them an ultimatum, or they got in trouble at work and were told to go to therapy or lose their job.

But on the rare occasion that I do get to work with them, the goal is to first gain their trust. Next is to work toward helping them open up about their early childhood. It is likely trauma occurred, to some degree. At any rate, my goal is actually to empower someone with Narcissism. I know it sounds odd, but Narcissism is really the result of extreme insecurity.

Under the incredible defense they display, they feel inadequate and are very sensitive to what others think about them. They are highly anxious and hyper-aware of other people's behavior around them as well as their own actions. Fear of rejection drives them to do anything possible to avoid it. The idea of "I'll hurt you before you hurt me" or "I'll leave you before you leave me" are common themes of a Narcissist, and wow, do they act on that. It's shocking sometimes at the logic they use to support their ideas and behavior, often leaving others dumbfounded, wondering what in the world just happened.

The Narcissist actually does desire affection, but they show restraint in relationships because they fear rejection. I help teach them about vulnerability and how to gain a sense of trust in one person, maybe two. Then, we work from there to learn to read an audience and try to understand how other people receive their behavior. Recognizing what behavior draws people to them and what behavior pushes people away is helpful for the Narcissist to learn. Typically, once I can crack that shell of armor, I find a very hurt and fragile person. Then the work begins.

How do you know if your partner is Narcissistic? The following red flags may be helpful. Narcissists:

- Keep their distance from others unless they need something, or a relationship will serve them or make them look good. But a loving, open, compassionate partnership with a Narcissist is hard to come by.

- Don't require human connection. They are shut down emotionally, especially when hurt. This is called a Narcissistic injury because when it happens to a narcissist, they will seek revenge.

- Are more comfortable when arguing. It's better to be angry and defensive than vulnerable and exposed.

- Are very good at gaslighting their partner.

- Have a high need for admiration.

- Are controlling and jealous.

- Tend to have unreasonable expectations for others to meet their own needs.

- Take advantage of others to achieve their personal needs.

- Are charming and confident, take the lead, and make the decisions.

- Are very intense sexual partners.

- Are master manipulators.

- Are likely to get into a relationship with people with low self-esteem and people-pleasing traits. This is a very dangerous combination for a relationship.

FEARFUL OR DISORGANIZED ATTACHMENT PERSONALITY TYPES: BORDERLINE CHARACTERISTICS LOOK LIKE THE FOLLOWING:

1. Frantic efforts to avoid real or imagined abandonment. Note: Do not include suicidal or self-mutilating behavior covered in Criterion 5

2. A pattern of unstable and intense interpersonal relationships characterized by alternating between extremes of idealization and devaluation

3. Identity disturbance: markedly and persistently unstable self-image or sense of self

4. Impulsivity in at least two areas that are potentially self-damaging (e.g., excessive spending, substance abuse, sex, reckless driving, binge eating). Note: Do not include suicidal or self-mutilating behavior covered in Criterion 5

5. Recurrent suicidal behavior, gestures, or threats, or self-mutilating behavior

6. Affective instability due to a marked reactivity of mood (e.g., intense episodic dysphoria, irritability, or anxiety usually lasting a few hours and only rarely more than a few days)

7. Chronic feelings of emptiness

8. Inappropriate, intense anger or difficulty controlling anger (e.g., frequent displays of temper tantrums, constant anger, and reoccurring fights)

9. Transient, stress-related paranoid ideation or severe dissociative symptoms (American Psychiatric Association, 2013)

Ways to strengthen the sense of self with Borderline Personality:

People exhibiting Borderline Personality are sometimes the most difficult to work with because they are anxious and dismissive. They want help, but they avoid personal ownership, and once they realize they must take ownership, they become defensive and usually stop therapy. I have been "fired" as a therapist by a handful of clients who were diagnosed with Borderline Personality.

When I do get the opportunity to really dig into what lies under the surface with these clients though, there is usually a great deal of trauma from childhood. As explained in the story of Angie, she suffered physical, emotional, and sexual abuse. Her ability to trust people and her environment was severely compromised. She wanted desperately to connect with people, almost in a dependent way, but she was scarred so badly that all she knew how to do was retreat. These traumatic issues have not been successfully processed and worked through. Any trigger that is slightly related to the trauma will ignite a trauma response, which will come out as rage, or they will completely cut off the connection. As with the other Personality Types, it is important for Borderline Personalities to create a strong internal sense of self, improve confidence, develop healthy coping mechanisms during conflict, and learn to build healthy relationships with people. Because addiction is common, addressing and treating this is an important part of therapy as well.

Dialectic Behavioral therapy is most common and specific for people with Borderline Personality. It is focused on teaching emotional regulation. The goals of therapy are to gain awareness and to be an observer of feelings before acting on them.

How do you know if your partner is Borderline? The following red flags may helpful. Borderlines:

- Make mountains out of molehills

- Have lots of abandonment issues

- Are impulsive and change moods quickly

- Use threats of self-harm and suicide for attention; they likely don't follow through, or the harm is superficial, but you should never dismiss this

- Have a past history of many short-term unhealthy relationships, usually sexual

- Are usually unfaithful to their partner

- Do not take responsibility for their actions but blame other people

- Give you hope they're changing, but their changes are short-lived

- Block themselves when they get emotionally too close, leading to a push-pull dynamic

- Exhibit lack of emotional regulation, including low stress tolerance and explosive anger

- Often make you feel responsible for their behavior because of manipulation and twisting thoughts

- Sabotage positive interactions

SELF-REFLECTION

In your journal, take some time to answer these questions thoughtfully. Feel free to elaborate. The more you write, the more personal you will make your experience:

- What is my Attachment Style?

- What is my Personality Type?

- What about my Attachment Style and Personality Type work for me in my life, and what causes more chaos?

- What do I want to change about my Attachment Style and Personality Type?

- What Attachment Style and Personality Type do I expect from a partner?

CHAPTER 4:
Four Communication Styles and Five Ways to Manage Conflict

PICTURE THIS. YOU'RE SITTING on your couch, in your home, a place of stability and comfort. Next to you sits a person you deeply care about, someone you are usually excited to share your time with. But today, your perspectives on a certain topic differ. You see it one way and are pretty set in your vision, and that person sees it a completely different way. Tensions are high, and you find yourselves raising voices and interrupting each other. You wonder, *What in the world are they thinking? If only they could hear me out, they will change their mind and my moment will become peaceful once more.* So, you keep talking at each other, but no one is listening, and the ability to have a successful dialogue is lost.

It could have been such an easy conversation to have, but instead, the tone gets louder, defenses are up, tempers flare, and things get said that can never be taken back. Doors slam, and finally, there is silence. But in your mind, the argument rolls around like granules of sand in the bottom of a rough ocean. Totally exhausted, you replay what you said and what your partner said, and you fall asleep and start the next day as if nothing happened. Does any of this sound familiar? Have you ever been a character in this movie?

Even though the sun sets and the sun rises, we don't get to clean-slate our emotions and act as if World War III didn't almost occur the night before. Too many of these situations and the relationship will fall on rocky grounds. Unresolved issues lead to resentment, and resentment leads to the end of a loving relationship.

Communication constitutes the majority of a relationship. Visualize the aspect of communication as a large umbrella, and its counterparts are body language, tone, presentation, eye contact, validation, defensiveness, just to name a few. We can't have a relationship without communication, and because there is no such thing as a perfect relationship, we also can't have one without conflict—a very important aspect of communication.

As we have discussed in the first three chapters, the experiences from childhood shape who you become in adulthood. The way you learned how to communicate your needs and how to deal with difficulty was role modeled to you as a child. Communication and conflict resolution influence and affect every relationship in your life, including friendships, acquaintances, romantic relationships—basically any relationship requiring vulnerability.

In my private practice, I can immediately predict if a couple I am working with will be successful in their relationship, based on how they talk with each other and how they resolve conflict. When a couple lacks direct conversation, they risk creating assumptions, which can lead to resentments, which is the ultimate cause of the death of a relationship.

Funny, but not funny, the song my ex-husband and I danced to at our wedding was Alison Krauss' "When You Say Nothing at All." I look back and chuckle because the death of our relationship was a complete lack of communication. My ex would just stare at me and say nothing in our arguments, which would send me through the roof, which would shut him down even more. I still love the song, but really Alison, maybe the title could have been "When You Say a Little Something." Oh well. Lesson learned.

The way we communicate encourages either a defensive response or an open, inviting response. The four Communication Styles are Passive, Passive-Aggressive, Aggressive, and Assertive. In this chapter, we will discuss how these Communication Styles are demonstrated based on the five ways of managing conflict: the Avoidant, Peacekeeper, My Way or the Highway, Compromiser, and Collaborator Styles.

Problems, negativity, and conflict. You may wonder why, throughout this book, I focus most on what happens when chaos arises. It's not that I am an eternal pessimist, but our greatest opportunity for growth happens during struggles. I guess that is because if everything were great all the time, we wouldn't need coping mechanisms or ways to deal with difficulty. But that isn't life. I've taught myself that when things are going well, enjoy this time because it won't last forever. On the flip side, when things are going badly, I utilize the tools I've learned to deal with the adversity, but I remind myself to hang in there, because, as they say, this too shall pass. Learning how we communicate and cope during these stressful times will help you ease the anxiety and help you feel empowered, even when you feel compromised.

This diagram depicts the ways we communicate to others, which changes in certain situations and around certain people. We behave differently when we are comfortable versus when we are intimidated or emotionally attacked. When we are confident, we do not question our voice nor our internal strength, but when we are emotionally or physically threatened, our worth is severely compromised. The goal is to be assertive in every situation. Stand up for yourself. That is where your pillar of strength lies.

To help you understand and ingrain the different Communication Styles, I will reference the characters of the popular movie *Ferris Bueller's Day Off* to describe this concept.

MODULE 4-
COMMUNICATION STYLES

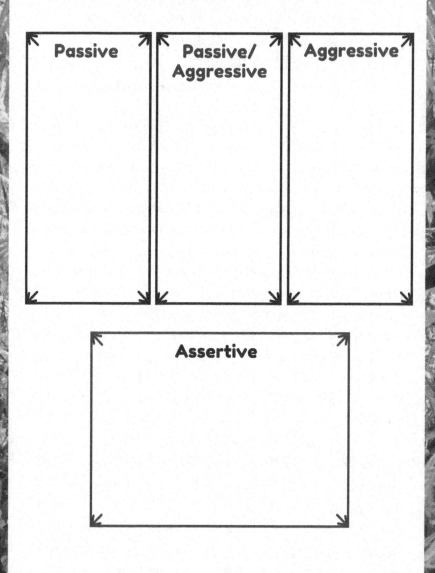

Passive

**Passive/
Aggressive**

Aggressive

Assertive

PASSIVE

> "If they aren't treating you right, it's
> time to stop blaming them. You decide
> your worth, so if you don't want to be a
> doormat, get off the floor."

–Charles Orlando

As a therapist, I think it is important to go back through your life and understand the *why* behind your behavior. However, I also encourage all my clients to stop and look at where they stand in the present. Own your behavior, and if you don't like it, you are the only one that can change it. Now is the time. So as the quote by Charles Orlando states, "get off the floor."

Passive behavior is often compared to being a doormat. Passivity is indicated by a slouching posture, with shoulders rolled forward. Eye contact is anywhere but directly with the person they are communicating with. When talking with someone who is passive, you might find yourself saying, "What?" because they talk so quietly and softly. A passive person apologizes consistently, usually for things that they had nothing to do with.

In *Ferris Bueller's Day Off*, Cameron Frye, played by Alan Ruck, exhibits the passive role perfectly. Cameron is a depressed, anxious teenager. He lacks confidence in himself and is easily manipulated into doing things he doesn't want to do. He is empathetic toward others and good-hearted but also avoids taking risks, possibly out of a fear of failure or getting out of his comfort zone. As the movie progresses, we learn Cameron feels very disconnected from his father, who seems to love his prize-possession car more than he loves Cameron. Cameron's feelings of rejection are likely the cause of his depression and anxiety. But, as passive as he is, Cameron just can't contain his anger forever, and toward the end of the movie, he flies into a rage, completely destroying the car.

You may not think passive type people lose their tempers the way Cameron did. However, humans are not robots, and emotion, especially built up, must go somewhere. Once it gets to a certain level, people either internally stuff their feelings or externally express them, whether they want to or not. Humans do not have a delete button to empty the feelings, never to be seen again. No, we can only take so much negativity. When these emotions go untouched, they build to dangerous levels. If they do keep the feelings inside, people typically experience anxiety, depression, illness, lack of sleep, or significant weight gain or loss, to name a few. If these undealt with emotions build, they could be externally expressed with rage and impulsive, highly charged actions. This usually catches people by surprise because the passive person is usually mild-mannered and quiet.

Being in a relationship with a passive person:

It's hard to tell where a passive person stands on issues. What do they really like or dislike? Where do they see their lives going? What do they want in a relationship?

Passive people can take on a victim mentality, feeling like bad things just keep happening to them. They often feel like they don't have any control over their lives. This can cause their partner to take the lead role, caring for the passive person. The partner can take on a sense of guilt as if they caused the problem. This can also be frustrating for the partner, who will lose respect and have resentment for the passive person.

When a passive person finds themselves in a relationship with an aggressive partner, which is a common connection, they create an unhealthy dance. While the passive dance partner slips into helplessness, the aggressive person becomes more controlling. The dance they do becomes a dance of extremes. Over time, the passive person loses themselves, and the aggressive person becomes superior and self-righteous.

Arguments with a passive person usually fizzle out quickly without a balanced resolution. The passive person will give in, compromising what they really want. The other person won't know what the passive person needs because it is never spoken. Unresolved arguments will persist and damage the relationship.

Think back to Chapter 2 when we discussed Family Roles and Chapter 3 when we discussed Attachment Styles and Personality Types. Where do you think the passive person would fit? The passive person would likely assume the Enabler role, morphing into what others wanted them to be, losing themselves, becoming a shell of a person. They would likely display the Anxious Attachment with the tagline "I need you" and display the Dependent Personality of being completely reliant on someone else to meet their needs. See how the puzzle pieces are fitting together?

AGGRESSIVE

> "The loudest one in the room is the weakest one in the room."
>
> **—Frank Lucas**

Aggressive people can be quite intimidating, but that is by design. The mentality of an aggressive person is that it's easier to be angry and guarded with their claws out than to be vulnerable, naked, and scared in the middle of a crowded room. The more they can intimidate by posturing their body and using large hand gestures, the better they feel about themselves for a moment. Aggressive people have no problem violating your personal space, even pointing their finger close to your nose. Their eyes will peer sharply right into yours as if they are trying to climb inside your head. Their tone of voice is as sharp as their claws projected out. It is difficult to finish your sentences because an aggressive person isn't interested in listening. Instead, you get interrupted anytime you try to speak.

Aggressive people are honest, and you know exactly how they feel, but the delivery is harsh and demeaning. They come across as self-righteous and controlling to overcompensate for their unassured sense of self. Because of this delivery, they don't feel listened to, which makes them become even more aggressive. If only they would recognize they are causing this whole chain reaction, the conversation may be different. But they don't even see how they don't give others a chance to have a dialogue because aggressive types tend to monopolize the situation.

The aggressive person may appear like the incredible hulk, but under all that scary exterior is an incredible amount of insecurity, fears of what people are thinking about them, and fears of rejection and abandonment. God forbid they ever tap into that because even the admission that it exists freaks them out too much, so we are left with the aggressive behavior to deal with.

In the movie *Ferris Bueller's Day Off*, our aggressive character is none other than Mr. Rooney, the Dean of Students at Glenbrook North High School. Played by Jeffrey Jones, Mr. Rooney is described as cold, strict, and unable to manage his anger. He abuses his power and treats the teachers and students with disrespect. Mr. Rooney is jealous of Ferris because he is so popular, while Mr. Rooney knows his staff and students don't like him.

The angrier Mr. Rooney gets, the more he makes horrible decisions, like breaking and entering Ferris' home. Eventually, his aggression gets the best of him, and he gets arrested.

Although this is a fictional movie, you probably know people who lean toward aggressive behavior. The way they manage strong emotion is by impulsively reacting. They may hear part of the story but lack patience to understand the full picture because they lose their tempers quickly. Although aggressive people lash out, sometimes afterward they feel a sense of guilt, but the ego prevents them from sincerely apologizing. As long as they refuse to admit they have a problem, the aggressive person is unlikely to change.

Being in a relationship with an aggressive person:

If you find yourself in a relationship with an aggressive type, you will either match that aggression, which can be highly volatile, or you're forced to take a more passive role and eventually become a shell of a person. These are the only two outcomes. It is next to impossible to maintain a healthy state of stability when you are up against this abusive behavior over a long period of time. You may feel humiliated, on guard, resentful, and scared.

Arguing with an aggressive person is a no-win situation. They will continue to escalate with physical, mental, emotional, and verbal attacks until the other person backs down. The conversation is usually filled with tangents. That's because the aggressive person is so out of control mentally, and the only tool they have to protect themselves is to lash out, grasping at whatever they can to feel they have won. The other person should usually remove themselves from this situation because there is probably not an option to find solutions.

Can you identify the Family Role, Attachment Style, and Personality Type? Likely, the aggressive person plays the role of the Scapegoat, sometimes the Family Hero. The Attachment Style is Avoidant, and the Personality Type is Narcissistic. An aggressive person also has traits of Borderline or Narcissistic personality.

PASSIVE AGGRESSIVE

> "Passive Aggression—Being covertly spiteful with the intent of inflicting mental pain."
>
> **—Ashta-Deb**

It would be a lot easier if passive-aggressive people came with a road map so you could follow the twisted web they weave. A passive-aggressive person will outwardly agree with something, but in all reality, they disagree. Instead of voicing their opinion, they will subtly go behind the scenes and sabotage the situation. For example, if someone is in a work group collectively working on a project and the passive-aggressive person doesn't agree with the project, they won't come right out and verbalize their dislikes. Instead, they may be late on deadlines or produce misinformation, so the project fails. They may not show up to team meetings or waltz in twenty minutes late, just to cause a disruption. However, to add on to the confusion, the passive-aggressive person will blame people around them instead of owning their behavior. This can leave people frustrated and confused, sometimes questioning their own intuition and the facts of a situation.

If the passive-aggressive person feels slighted, instead of being direct about how they feel, they will secretly plan revenge to feel better. Instead of confronting the person they have an issue with, they will go behind their back, gossiping and creating sides. They can behave very bitter and hostile toward people but are reluctant to call out the elephant in the room, so to speak. Being direct is not in the passive-aggressive person's nature.

Under the surface of the passive-aggressive person is a great deal of insecurity. They feel everyone is against them and feel unappreciated. They carry resentments about past situations and people who have done them wrong, not seeing what their own contribution could have been. This leads to many unresolved issues.

Their body language can be shifty, and their eye contact aloof. Their tone is ladened with sarcasm. It may seem like everything is fine and as if they don't care about the situation at hand, while there is a hint of anger sprinkled throughout. Their words are not direct and clear but spoken under their breath, just loud enough to hear, but soft enough that you only catch a couple of words, which keeps you guessing about what their next move may be.

Our character who is passive-aggressive in the *Ferris Bueller* film is Ferris' sister, Jeanie, played by Jennifer Grey. Jeanie is extremely jealous of Ferris because he gets away with everything he does. She is seething as she watches the school day unfold, Ferris having a great time, and all the students showering her brother with love. This motivates her to develop a plot to seek revenge against him. Because of her jealousy, Jeanie's aggression and sarcasm are displayed toward her parents, the dean, Mr. Rooney, and the school secretary, Grace. When Jeanie ends up at the police station and meets an inmate with whom she falls in love after he gives her some positive attention, he even tells her, "The problem with you is that you need to worry more about yourself than others." Falling for a guy the second he gave her any attention is an example of her insecurities.

Externally, she displays a judgmental, uncompromising type of character. Later in the movie, we see that Jeanie actually cares for her brother and ends up covering for him so he doesn't get into trouble. While her rage was initially focused on getting revenge on her brother, who seems to lead a consequence-free life, she eventually turns her vengeance toward Mr. Rooney as he is the one responsible for not catching Ferris in all his antics. When Mr. Rooney gets attacked by the dog, Jeanie smiles through her passive-aggressive enjoyment. She was indirectly involved in the dog attacking him (passive), didn't stop the dog from attacking (aggressive), and enjoyed the aftermath of the event (got her need met through manipulation).

Jeanie has more of the "aggressive" than the "passive," but her jealousy, sarcasm, and revenge-seeking behavior fit her into the passive-aggressive category.

Passive-aggressive people will give you the silent treatment and keep you wondering what they are thinking. To feel a sense of control, they will strive to determine if and when others will find a resolution to a conflictual situation. Their confidence is low while insecurities are high.

Being in a relationship with a passive-aggressive person:

All I can say is keep a baggie of breadcrumbs so you can find your way back to a state of peace. It can be exhausting because you just don't have a clear understanding of what they are thinking or feeling. You will likely apologize for actions that are not your fault, which will deteriorate your confidence and self-worth. Be careful not to personalize what is happening. I'd almost guarantee that the passive-aggressive person was like this way before you entered the picture. It is likely you are not the only one receiving this treatment. It's important to have good boundaries if you find yourself here.

Arguments with a passive-aggressive person can turn into mind-twisting events. The tactic of the passive-aggressive person is to throw off their opponent by manipulating words and perceptions. Here is a figurative example of how a passive-aggressive person operates. Visualize the passive-aggressive person carefully gathering twigs and logs to build a perfect fire—this is the situation. Then, they quietly and secretly light the fire—manipulation. When the other person responds with anger and/or desperation—this is the reaction from the victim of the passive-aggressive person—the passive-aggressive person steps back and blames everyone for being so out of control. And that is what passive-aggression looks like.

Can you identify the Family Role, Attachment Style, and Personality Type? If you guessed the Fearful or Disorganized Attachment Style and Borderline Personality Type, you are probably correct. As for the Family Role, it could be the Enabler or Scapegoat.

ASSERTIVE

"To be passive is to let others decide for you. To be aggressive is to decide for others. To be assertive is to decide for yourself. And to trust that there is enough, that you are enough."

— Edith Eva Eger

The assertive method of communicating is the goal. This is going to be the most healthy, effective Communication Style. The body language of an assertive person is alert, shoulders down and back; eye contact is direct. The tone of voice is calm and clear. Assertive people are direct and firm, and they speak with compassion. They respect themselves and others. They are confident in what they need in their lives and are independent, trusting themselves to make good decisions. Of course, assertive people have conflict in their lives and struggle from time to time. Conflicts that arise are the typical life bumps in the road, but assertive people do not invite conflict into their lives the way the other communicative types do. When they need to ask for help, they aren't afraid to. Working as a team and resolving issues are part of the normal path for the assertives.

The character in the *Ferris Bueller* film who most represents the Assertive communicator is, of course, Ferris, played by Matthew Broderick. Ferris knows exactly what he wants, who he wants to hang out with, what he wants to do, and how he's going to do it. He is confident and not afraid to step out of his comfort zone. A couple of times in the movie, when Ferris thinks he might have crossed the line with his actions, he has an empathetic response. One example was in the cab ride downtown. While skipping school, Cameron, Sloane, and Ferris were taking a taxi to their next grand event. Ferris looked over to the cab next to them, and there was his father! He appeared to be scared that he was caught lying to his dad and that they'd get in trouble for skipping school, that his parents would be disappointed in him, and that his friends would get caught doing something he talked them into. He also showed kindness when Cameron destroyed his father's car, knowing his friend was going to have some major consequences. Ferris showed worry and guilt during these clips, demonstrating true compassion for his friends. He recognizes when Cameron is down in the dumps, and he comes over to cheer him up and get him out of bed, demonstrating empathy. Granted, Ferris used manipulation and dishonesty in the movie to get some needs met (assertive people don't usually use those tactics), but otherwise, his character fits the assertive category. Like other assertive people, he's encouraging, level-headed, self-reliant, even-tempered, unselfish, and likeable.

Being in a relationship with an assertive person:

Being in a relationship with an assertive person feels very natural and easygoing. The work in this relationship is to continue to communicate and change with the normal dynamics of a relationship. Conflict will occur, but an assertive person will want to understand your perspective, offer validation, and work with you to create a resolution. They are willing to listen to other perspectives and will apologize when they're wrong. Because of their strong self-confidence, assertive people don't view apologizing as a weakness, but they know it takes courage to admit fault. They have appropriate boundaries with others. Assertive people won't likely stay in toxic relationships, so if you are with an assertive person, you must have assertive traits as well.

Arguing with an assertive person is almost impossible. They are not reactive, not trying to prove themselves, or fearful of being taken advantage of. If someone tries to instigate or pick a fight with an assertive person, it will lose the spark and fizzle out. The assertive person will use their firm but compassionate nature to identify the problem, hear the other person, offer validation, and then state their own position. They don't use fighting words to escalate. That is not the goal of the assertive person. The goal is to honor and respect themselves, therefore, honoring and respecting those around them.

What are the Family Role, Attachment Style, and Personality Type of the assertive person? They are likely the Family Hero with Secure Attachment and no real personality dysfunction.

RECOGNITION IS THE KEY

We all have experienced times of being passive, aggressive, and passive-aggressive. Every single one of us has, so don't get down on yourself if you see personal traits in each category. First remember, recognition is the key step to changing something that causes you problems in your life. Second, there is not one perfect person out there. We all have room to change our ways and have plenty of chances to continue our growth down the road. What I want to emphasize here is that if you see a consistent pattern in your life of chaos and difficulty, you might identify that you bring some of it on yourself. Understanding the *why* behind the behavior is, again, where your goldmine of opportunity to change lies.

What does being passive, aggressive, passive-aggressive, or assertive have to do with managing conflict? Well, what do you think the success rate is to resolve conflict in each of these Communication Styles? All except assertive are likely to result in unresolved issues, a lack of trust in the relationship, and increased resentment. They are likely to have frequent arguments because all the hurt feelings lie festering below the surface, and it doesn't take much to ignite them.

Think of the last conflict you had at work, or at home, or with a friend. It is common to have different ways of dealing with the disruption depending on who's on the other end. Do you notice that you act differently in different settings? Are you more passive around authority? Are you more passive-aggressive around people who are intimidating to you? Are you more aggressive with people you look down on? Are you more assertive with people who you respect and feel comfortable with? Interesting how we can change our approach, knowing that being assertive is the best way to communicate and solve a tough situation.

The way you communicate your needs is based on how confident you feel. Confidence is a major factor. When you are confident, you're likely to be more assertive. When you are questioning yourself and lacking confidence, you impulsively reach for other ways to get your point across. In any relationship, the ability to be confident and speak freely is crucial. We'll dip into this in Chapter 6.

FIVE CONFLICT MANAGEMENT STYLES

> "Ten percent of conflict is due to difference in opinion, and 90 percent is due to delivery and tone of voice."
>
> **—Herbert Henry Lehman**

MODULE 4- CONFLICT MANAGEMENT STYLES

AVOIDANT

PEACEKEEPER

MY WAY OR THE HIGHWAY

COLLABORTOR

COMPROMISER

Here you see five ways that people manage a situation that can cause their heart to beat out of their chest and smoke blow out of their ears. As you read through these methods, see if you can relate to any or all of these. Ask yourself how it worked out in the end. Would you have changed the outcome?

Each style you see provides effective and ineffective ways of managing conflict based on the given situation. Here I will define each style, connect it with a communication type, and tie it to an Attachment Style as discussed in Chapter 3 and to a Family Role from Chapter 2. As a reminder, how we were raised and what was role modeled to us has so much to do with our relationships with ourselves and with others.

Avoidant

I have a client; I'll call her Ruth. I have seen Ruth for about five months once a week. She originally came to me because she was a single mom and overwhelmed. She was having issues with her son, who was acting out at home and getting in trouble at school. Her daughter, who graduated from high school, didn't want to go to college and refused to get a job. Neither of her kids helped with chores around the house, and Ruth, working two jobs, took on the responsibility of everything herself. She felt resentful toward the kids, but she continued to cook, clean, pay the bills, and not address any of it.

At times, her daughter was so defiant that she would punch holes in her bedroom wall when Ruth would get on her to help out around the house. Both kids were demanding, but she continued to enable the behavior by avoiding taking a stand and setting boundaries. You see, Ruth has a history of getting into abusive relationships. She was emotionally and sexually abused as a child, never received any therapy to deal with the trauma, and now avoids conflict throughout her life. She continues to get into abusive relationships with men.

With her children, Ruth pretends nothing is wrong, that she is managing just fine. But a person can take only so much. When she just can't take picking up that last dirty dish out of her son's room, she uses guilt and sarcasm to express her frustration. She's lost all respect from her kids, and her daughter just laughs and rolls her eyes.

At work, Ruth feels the most in control of her life. But recently, her supervisor changed her schedule around, putting her on weekend shifts without even asking if she was okay with it. Ruth ran to her coworker, ranted and raved to her about her supervisor, and then called in sick for the next shift, leaving the staff short-handed. She never addressed the issue with her supervisor. Instead, Ruth did the bare minimum at work and ended up getting fired.

In therapy, we have been talking about why Ruth is avoidant and uses passive-aggressive ways to get her point across. She is beginning to see how all the unresolved issues revolve around the trauma from her past. Avoidance has helped keep Ruth comfortable, but being comfortable is not always being healthy. Teaching Ruth to develop boundaries with others, find her voice, and improve her confidence while also working through trauma is the goal of therapy. It's taken her years to get to where she is now, so I'm hoping she will be patient with herself as she takes the time to become more empowered.

Ruth's communication type is passive-aggressive. Her Attachment Style is Fearful/Disorganized, and she has Borderline personality traits. Her Family Role was likely the Lost Child and Enabler.

There is a good time to use the Avoidant management style, however. Say you are in a situation where you really don't care about the relationship or the topic you're avoiding. For example, what if you were reading an article online, say, about the latest political upset. As you read people's comments, you feel your blood pressure rise as you disagree with what they write. Okay, you care about the topic, but you couldn't care less about who is expressing their opinion. If you react and write something out of anger, what will that do for you? Are you seriously thinking you'll change the opinion of this total stranger? This may be a situation where avoidance is your best bet. You decide you are glad you aren't having this total stranger with completely opposite political opinions over for dinner tonight. You log out of that commentary, go kiss your dog, and move on with your day. Avoidance here saved you from being angry and likely taking your negative emotions out on someone around you in that moment who you actually do care about.

Peacekeeper

I will use a client of mine who I'll call Evy to describe the peacekeeper role. Evy is the sweetest, most empathetic person, but she has completely lost herself. Evy is twenty-eight years old and has lived her life doing what other people want her to do. I don't think she has ever even asked herself what she wants in her life. Because her confidence is next to nonexistent, she has never had a job or gotten her driver's license, creating a complete dependence on her family to take care of her. She avoided conflict like the plague.

When Evy went to college, just around the corner from her house, she met a man who she was very attracted to. She formed an instant attachment to him because he took the role of a caretaker with his confidence and charm. As lovely as she thought this relationship would be, the new beau just took the place of her parents, and she found herself in the same passive role. They moved in together rather quickly. Evy came to therapy because her friends and family expressed concern about this new relationship of hers. She hardly ever leaves the house; she waits for this guy—let's call him Sam—to come home. During the day, she waits by her phone for him to call or return her text messages. Evy has developed an addiction to this relationship. It's as if Sam will complete who she is. She relies on him to make her happy and to feel worthy. Sam is starting to put his guard up because the qualities he was initially attracted to, her kind heart and the fact that she'd do anything for him, were quickly turning into pressure to fulfill a task that's impossible for him to succeed at, which then makes Evy confident.

Evy is lying to her friends and her parents about how she is taking care of herself because she doesn't want them to worry. She agrees with everything Sam wants to do because she doesn't want to upset him. All the while, she is falling apart inside.

As Sam disengages from Evy because of the pressure he feels to make her happy and content, Evy becomes more and more anxious, creating a vicious cycle. The goals of therapy with me are to improve Evy's self-worth. She is adding things to her life that she is in control of: a job, expanding her social circle, finding her voice, and setting short-term, realistic goals for what she wants in her life. When she sets a goal and achieves it, Evy is ecstatic. This is slowly but surely building her confidence. The relationship with Sam was doomed from the beginning, based on the unhealthy foundation it was developed from. Although Sam is now out of the picture, Evy is learning to feel more empowered within before she seeks out a new romantic partner.

Evy's Attachment Style is Anxious, and she developed a Dependent personality. Her Communication Style is Passive, and the way she manages conflict is by making sure everyone is happy, at the cost of her own happiness.

Being the Peacekeeper has its place in managing conflict. Sometimes keeping the relationship is more important than losing it. Pick your battles, but don't overuse this method of dealing with difficult issues because you'll lose yourself and lose respect and credibility with others. An example of a beneficial time to keep the peace is going to dinner with your partner. You really feel like Italian, but you settle for Chinese food. You don't speak up about your desire for Italian, but at that time, you're really okay with Chinese. No harm, no foul. You figure this weekend you'll get the Italian food you crave.

My Way or the Highway

I would now like to introduce you to a client of mine I will call Rob. Rob entered therapy with me because his marriage is on the line. His wife has threatened to leave him after a seven-year relationship. I've had about ten sessions with

Rob so far, and it wasn't until the fourth session that he started to admit some of his contributions to his failing marriage. During the first three sessions, Rob was angry about being forced to come to therapy, talked about how his boss was an idiot, his wife nagged him all the time, and my office was out of his way. I listened to him complain about all of the people he thought were stupid and took up his time in his life. I worked to create a safe space for Rob to come in and vent until he began to personally attack me. I had to set firm limits with him on what was acceptable. I encouraged him to dig down to locate the real reasons he was coming to therapy and reminded him that unless he looked in the mirror and was willing to work on himself, he would lose his job and the love of his life. I asked him to think about what he wanted from counseling, and in his next sessions, he switched gears from blaming everyone around him for his unhappiness to owning his behavior and making small shifts.

Rob decided to return to my office for therapy and, slowly but surely, he opened up about areas he used bullying and intimidation with many people in his life. He found that aggression and attacking were his go-to's when he was intimidated or felt someone was criticizing him. Even though he could open up in his sessions with me, Rob has a hard time implementing what he was learning in therapy. He is making progress, but only because he is willing to learn and change. Because of the aggressive, demeaning behavior he displayed in his relationship, the ability to trust and respect each other was whittled down to a bare minimum and will take time to restore. At work, Rob was able to develop healthy coping mechanisms when conflict was presented and has been able to keep his job. However, his self-centered behavior has been ingrained over time and will take time and persistence on his part to change.

Rob's Attachment Style is Avoidant. He has Narcissistic personality traits, and the way he has managed conflict is with Aggression. In learning more about Rob, I'd say he fits the Hero and the Scapegoat Family Role.

There is a time when the My Way or the Highway management style is appropriate. But you want to use this very sparingly because shutting people down will result in them feeling unsafe and not being valued. An example of when to use this could be when you have to take control over a dangerous situation. Say you are with a group of people, and there is a tornado warning. You must make a fast decision to pack up. People are panicking, not thinking clearly, dilly-dallying around, and not knowing what to do. Telling the group that you don't care what they think and that we are leaving now or we're going to die would make sense.

Compromiser

There are times when decisions need to be made and not everyone can get their way. This is when compromising takes place. I have provided therapy to a client I will call Pam. She recently lost her grandfather and was co-planning the funeral services. Working with her family and close friends was causing her stress because everyone wanted the funeral services their way. Some people wanted it at a beach destination, while others wanted it in the mountains with snow-capped peaks. Since her grandfather hadn't spoken his wishes, Pam was trying to accommodate everyone during such a difficult time.

Compromising is working to find a solution for all sides. Each side picks the things that they are willing to give up. In order to make this successful, each side has to know their limits and what they are *actually* willing to give up or they could feel resentful. Each side also has to have trust in the other side for honestly developing this list of what they are actually "willing" to give up instead of just creating what may not have been important in the first place. When compromising, there is a risk of being manipulated by the other side.

In Pam's case, she evaluated what her family wanted and knew they couldn't hold services at a beach and in the snow. She decided to find a beautiful lake where people could be by the water but also drive to hiking opportunities, reaching a snowy destination.

For Pam to be able to make this decision, she had to be secure in herself and able to set limits, but in a compassionate way. Based on these facts, her Attachment Style is Secure, her Communication Type is Assertive, and her Family Role is likely Hero with Enabling traits.

This Conflict Management style is encouraged when all parties must give something up to come to an agreement.

Collaborator

The last conflict resolution style is Collaborator. This is similar to Compromiser, but instead of having to give things up, every person involved gets their way. It is a win-win outcome for all.

A situation that many people can relate to is around schools and the COVID-19 pandemic. If you have kids or know people who have kids, returning to school has been a scheduling nightmare for school districts: Do we return to school or stay at home? In order to make this decision and accommodate everyone, the districts sent out surveys to all the families asking what they wanted their kids to do. They gathered all the information and evaluated the needs. This required the decision-makers to have an open discussion and listen to all perspectives. Then they needed to get creative and find options to meet everyone's needs. The compromise was to do online school for the first two weeks and then give families the option to have their kids come to school part-time or stay home and do online school full-time. This seemed to meet the requests from families.

This is an example of Collaborating to manage conflict. It requires Secure Attachment and Assertive Communication, and this would fall under the Hero and Enabler Family Role.

SELF-REFLECTION

We have now explored the Communication Styles: Passive, Aggressive, Passive-Aggressive, and Assertive. We have also explored five ways to manage conflict. There are times when we have used each way of communicating and each method to deal with difficult situations.

At this time, I suggest that you evaluate your own experiences and situations. Some questions to journal around are the following:

- Do you recall times that you used a more passive approach and wished you'd been more assertive?

- How about a time you were more aggressive and lost a friend or ruined a relationship?

- What is your Communication Style?
  o In personal relationships? Does it work? What would you change?
  o In business relationships? Does it work? What would you change?

- What is your Conflict Resolution Style?
  o In personal relationships? Does it work? What would you change?
  o In business relationships? Does it work? What would you change?

- What do I want in my Communication and Conflict Management style to look like going forward?

- What Communication and Conflict Management style do I expect from a partner?

- What Communication and Conflict Management style have my past partners demonstrated?

CHAPTER 5:
The Cycles of Healthy and Toxic Conflict

"The toxic behaviors were there before you
decided to enter into relationships with
them. The signs were there. You may have
chosen to look the other way, but the signs
were there."

—P.A. Speers

THE OLD ME

WHEN I WAS IN my twenties, I stayed way too long in an abusive relationship. I was in my dependent personality phase. This relationship was built on extremes; either my heart was shooting off fireworks, or I was crumpled up and crying my eyes out on the floor. We were either off doing exciting excursions, or I was being yelled at, called names, and accused of behaviors—like having sex with random people—that I wouldn't have even dreamed of acting on. I'd build the courage to leave him. But then, with his sad puppy dog eyes, he'd say, "So this is it?" I believed I was responsible for his happiness, so I would compromise my worth and crawl back into such a toxic relationship. No matter how my friends and family warned me, no matter how many informational pamphlets on domestic violence my coworkers anonymously put in my mailbox, I stayed. The emotional mind-twisting and the irrational and erratic behavior got worse. Physical violence eventually worked its way into the relationship. But when I heard his apologies and watched how helpless he seemed, I felt an obligation to stay.

I didn't grow up in this type of environment, and I wondered how in the world I had found myself going around and around like I was in the crazy teacup ride at the carnival. The relationship I was in sure didn't start like that, but I had become a dizzy mess about a year in and stayed for another five years.

When the idea of violence is brought up, our first reaction is likely anger and disgust at the person inflicting the pain. However, it takes two people to make a healthy relationship, but it also takes two people to create an unhealthy and toxic relationship. I had to take a step back and ask myself, "What is my part? What am I doing to perpetuate this negativity? Why am I in this relationship, and why do I stay?" The ability to recognize your own responsibility is essential to moving forward and creating healthy patterns. Just to clarify, this does not mean that you can change the other person. You can only make changes within yourself.

The first six months of a relationship are, or should be, fantastic. You're aware of your actions, words, and behaviors while trying to impress each other. You're getting to know the other person, and you might not be as forthright with your feelings, your thoughts, or perspectives during this time. As a side note, if the first six months of a relationship are filled with fighting and chaos, I seriously encourage you to reevaluate the situation and consider getting out. Get a therapist and get help to understand aspects of yourself and why you are attracted to this type of behavior.

Six months is a rough estimate, but in my experience, I can always tell when I am working with couples around their six-month mark because that is when the first real conflict occurs. It is when those little things that you thought were kind of cute or maybe a little bit annoying become something that starts getting under your skin. This is the first opportunity to practice the conflict-resolution skills you bring with you into the relationship. It is also the time to evaluate how your partner is able to resolve conflict. You can tell a lot about a person based on how they handle their anger.

The more you get to know a person and see them in a variety of settings, the more information you are able to gather and evaluate. Taking time to grow a relationship allows you to be able to identify red flags or warning behaviors, identify communication patterns, and evaluate how they treat you around their friends and family and out in public.

Of the two methods to work through conflict, one is healthy, resulting in a greater connection with the other person, and one is toxic, resulting in unresolved issues and chaos. After I show you these cycles, I will introduce you to the new me.

When you think of conflict, you may notice a shift in your body, a heaviness. This happens because conflict is associated with negativity, sadness, hopelessness. However, I want to help you shift that idea because conflict can be a positive, relationship-building tool. "What?" you say. Yes. As you have learned, conflict is unavoidable in relationships. Think of it this way. You take two people, from two different upbringings, with two different personalities, and say, "Okay, you both are now together in a relationship for the rest of your life. Good luck." Of course, there will be disagreements, hurt feelings, and likely periods of time when you shut down from each other.

However odd it seems, times like that can enhance your relationship, and the *way* it is handled can increase trust and respect. Think back to when a conflict erupted within a romantic relationship you have or had. After the dust settled, do you remember feeling distanced and disconnected from the other person, or do you remember feeling sad that the argument happened but more connected and understood? Here it will become clear why you felt the way you did.

CYCLE OF HEALTHY CONFLICT

"The goal of resolving conflict in a relationship is not victory or defeat. It's understanding and letting go of our need to be right."

—Unknown

MODULE 4- CYCLE OF HEALTHY CONFLICT

Conflict

Time-out. Set specified time

Time-in Communication phase

Honeymoon, renewed intimacy

Real life, normal events that can be stressful

Here you see a pie chart of five phases of the Healthy Cycle of Conflict Management. We'll begin with the section about real-life events that create stress and tension. Normal stress happens: you have a bad day at work, get stuck in traffic on your way home, get home and see your dogs have gotten into the trash and created a mess for you to clean up. These life events can create frustration. When you are already frustrated by everyday inconveniences, one more chaotic event can be the tipping point that causes you to get snarky with your partner, even though they didn't have anything to do with your irritation. It's easy for stress to build, and then the emotions follow. You're short-tempered, and you exchange sharp words. Eventually, conflict will erupt.

In a healthy relationship, conflict looks like raised, stern voices, abrupt or mean things being said, even a door slamming. At some point, either person recognizes that the conversation isn't going in a healthy direction and calls for a Time-Out, which is just taking space. They respect each other enough to recognize that there is truth in this and allow the Time-Out to happen.

Time-Out and Time-In Stage

There are specific guidelines to an effective Time-Out.

1. Specify how long the Time-Out should last before checking in with each other. For example, you each agree that in thirty minutes, you will check in to see if you're ready to talk. If you are still so heated that an effective conversation is unlikely to occur, you request another thirty minutes. The reason for setting a time limit is based on how people communicate.

Some people—more often women than men—want to talk and talk and talk. They process as the words come out of their mouths. Other people—more often men—need to gather the information, let it simmer in their minds, organize the thoughts and feelings, and determine how they want to communicate it, and then they are ready to talk. If one person forces an opposite communication method on the other person, they are likely to find themselves right back into the conflict phase. Therefore, you need a Time-Out.

2. During the Time- Out, each person has an assignment.
    - Determine what the argument was really about. You know how when you argue with someone and many tangents grow like a wild vine in the jungle? When you finally take the Time-Out, you aren't even sure what you were fighting about in the first place. So, determining what the bottom line was is important.
    - What was the other person trying to tell you? This is the most important step of the Time-Out. This is when you put your own opinions on the back burner and determine what the other person was trying to tell you.
    - Now you can clear up what your opinion is regarding the argument. Most importantly, ask yourself *why* you had such a strong reaction. Where was it coming from?

3. When both people are calm, you come back together and decide who will get to talk first. This is the next section of the diagram, the Time-In stage. Remember, one person talks, and the other listens. The talker first starts with, "What I heard you saying was…." The talker is not repeating their own opinion. Instead, they are validating the other person. Validation is magic, and it's the fastest way to drop someone's defenses. When you validate someone, you communicate that their opinion is important, and you want to understand. By validating, you don't have to agree with the other person, but you do have to hear them. This is the most crucial step of the whole Time-In process because if defenses are high, it's impossible to communicate. We all want to be heard and listened to. It makes us feel respected. Validation also allows for clarification. What if you thought you heard what the other person's opinion was, but you were 100 percent wrong? Then you reacted to something that you misunderstood. How many times have you been there before? Me, plenty. Once validation and clarification have been established, the other person gets to talk. Congratulations, you are now having a dialogue instead of talking at each other.

I don't recommend taking a Time-Out for more than twenty-four hours. Not talking to your partner just allows more tension to build, which adds to further miscommunication. Furthermore, life continues to happen, and if you wait too long to discuss the elephant in the middle of the room, you may never get back to it, leading to unresolved issues, and you guessed it, resentment. Also, the sooner you call the Time-Out, the less time you need to calm down. If the argument got very heated and the anger and anxiety shot through the roof, it is going to take longer to calm down so that all that adrenaline and cortisol can be reabsorbed by your body. As you work to create the new habit of calling a Time-Out, you likely will wait too long. But over time, you will recognize when you need to take space. After developing a habit of learning to effectively communicate, you can learn to pause, collect your thoughts, and have a dialogue, sometimes in the moment, without even needing to separate from the other person to take space. It works.

Honeymoon/Renewed Intimacy Stage

Next is the Honeymoon/Renewed Intimacy stage. I actually think it is less of a Honeymoon, as you will learn in the Toxic Cycle of Conflict. But there is definitely Renewed Intimacy. Remember when I said that conflict can make people feel closer? You feel that in this stage. When Jim and I have an argument, we work it out, and I know he still loves me. He allows me to get my words out, even if he doesn't agree with me. He sees me at my less-than-finer moments, and he still accepts me for who I am. Now, there have been times where I've crossed that line and gone overboard. He'll call me out, but even then, we talk, I apologize for where I was out of line, and I still know he loves me. I do the same for him. Life isn't perfect. Relationships aren't perfect. But being able to recognize where you were wrong, and offering an honest and sincere apology, results in feeling even closer to your partner than you were before the conflict.

MODULE 5-
CYCLE OF TOXIC
CONFLICT

Conflict

Honeymoon

Tension

CYCLE OF TOXIC CONFLICT

> "Abusive relationships exist because they provide enough rations of warmth, laughter, and affection to clutch onto like a security blanket in the heap of degradation. The good times are the initial euphoria that keeps addicts draining their wallets for toxic substances to inject into their veins. Scraps of love are food for an abusive relationship."

—Maggie Young

This diagram is a picture of the Cycle of Toxic Conflict. As you see, it consists of only three sections. What's missing? There is no Time-Out or Time-In stage, and there is not a Renewed Intimacy stage. Let's break it down.

You see the normal life stress in the Tension stage. Same situation as we talked about earlier. You have a bad day at work, get stuck in traffic on your way home, get home and see your dogs have gotten into the trash and created a mess for you to clean up. What is different, is that you come home to your partner, with whom you already have unresolved issues from yesterday, last week, and last month. The tension isn't just about the day, is it? It's been building over time. Because there is no resolution, the tension is visible the minute you walk in the door.

There is your partner—no eye contact, no, "Hi honey, I'm glad you're home. How was your day?" Just silence. That same deafening, lonely silence reminding you of the anger and the harsh words that are likely just around the corner.

You feel it in the pit in your stomach, wondering if your partner will blow up tonight, or if maybe you can slink away and pretend you're sleeping like you did last night in order to avoid the wrath. But you move around the corner, your shoulder bag knocks the bottle of beer off the counter, and it spills all over the floor. "Dear God, no! Oh no!" Here comes the thunder.

Oh, the name-calling, the insults, the yelling, and the tone that just sits in your eardrum, echoing all the negative things about yourself. Based on your day and the long drive home, you decide to match this nonsense and yell back. The banter gets louder, and then, *crack*, you hear a bottle hit the wall right behind you. You grab your keys and your dog and head out the door to stay with your best friend. Finally, silence again.

As you see in the diagram, tensions from past, unresolved issues are just festering under the surface. It doesn't take much for the conflict to ignite. Within toxic conflict, verbal, emotional, mental, and/or physical abuse occurs. This can be demonstrated by name-calling, condescending remarks, manipulation, ignoring, pushing, shoving, hitting, and the list goes on. There is a lack of healthy coping mechanisms, and neither partner calls for space to calm down. Instead, in the toxic relationship, the conflict finally ends because of exhaustion or emergency intervention. Often during toxic conflict, alcohol or drugs are involved, resulting in one person passing out. What follows next is the Honeymoon.

You may wonder how on earth a Honeymoon could exist after that chaos. It is called a Honeymoon because it is completely opposite of the conflict, but the intention isn't celebration. The Honeymoon stage is based on fear. In the Honeymoon stage, one person, usually the one who inflicted the abusive behavior, realizes they lost control and are at risk of losing their partner.

The morning after your fight, you are at your best friend's house with your dog, and you receive a text message. It reads, "Good morning, baby. I miss you. I miss our dog. I'm sure he misses his bed, and I hope you miss yours. Last night was insane. You know I love you and couldn't imagine my life without you. If you aren't in my life, I am nothing. Please come home so I can wrap my arms around you and make everything better." Exactly the words you have been longing for. Finally, he gets it, he sees it, he's willing to change. So, you pack up your belongings, grab the dog, hug your bestie, and head home. When you arrive, he hugs you, and all seems to be okay. For now.

The Honeymoon is based on a sense of guilt, embarrassment, avoidance, and/or fear of consequences for their horrible display of abusive behavior. The partner who lost control of themselves is now overly nice to their partner. They shower the other person with apologies, compliments, and gifts. The victim in this situation can feel some validation, but they also question if they experienced the abusive behavior as bad as it was. They tend to justify the abuse, accept the apology, and seek to renew the relationship, just wanting to get back to a sense of calm.

Now, there was technically a Time-Out because you left out of fear and cried all night at your friend's house. But the Time-In didn't consist of any problem solving or validation. It was avoidance of ownership and avoidance of the trauma that occurred. What sits right below the surface is a complete lack of resolution and fear. As you see in the diagram, the tension phase repeats itself with normal tension but now with additional tension from all the unresolved issues. The conflict erupts, the Honeymoon period follows, and the cycle goes around and around. But resentment, distrust, and disrespect grow between the partners. They become guarded against each other. You may find yourself walking on eggshells and losing all respect. After too many of these instances, you will now see how the sections of the chart shift. Renewed Intimacy doesn't even have time to get established.

MODULE 5-
CYCLE OF TOXIC
CONFLICT

Honeymoon

Conflict

Tension

> "Revenge is surviving, getting out, and
> being a better person than you were, and
> breaking the cycle."

—Kristy Green

In this diagram, you see that conflict is starting to overtake the relationship. Fifty percent of the interactions are based in Conflict. As Maggie Young says, the relationship will continue because at least there is 25 percent of the Honeymoon to grasp onto.

The conflict doesn't always look like thrashing around and yelling at each other. Conflict can be passive, under the radar. It can be demonstrated by manipulation, twisting of words, applying meaning to emotions that do not exist. Conflict can be refusing to talk and conducting your life as if the other person doesn't even exist.

I have a client—I will call her Pam—I've been seeing for about four months now. Pam has been married for over twenty-five years. She holds a very prominent job, one you would envision for a strong, assertive woman who has zero tolerance for B.S. She is very successful at this job, but when she described her home life, I was taken aback by how passive she is. She talks about her husband, who dismisses her and has for almost as long as they've been married. He doesn't talk with her or ask how her day was. He doesn't include her in his plans. He demands his dinner and a clean house and lavish parties to entertain his colleagues. They have two boys together, now adults, who treat Pam the same way their father does.

She has described how one son has a girlfriend, and Pam watches her son repeat this dismissive, emotionally destructive cycle over again directed toward the girl-friend. Over the years, it is clear how Pam's confidence has diminished into dust. Her depression and anxiety are insurmountable. Pam has tried every medication and treatment available to try and relieve her symptoms. The one thing she hasn't tried is changing her environment. The conflict she experiences in her marriage isn't displayed in hateful words but through neglect.

In fact, I believe that when people are fighting and yelling, there is still an aspect of where they care about the relationship. Not that I encourage that because it is so emotionally costly. But when there is indifference, that is the ultimate relationship killer. When it is dead, there is no emotion. When Pam's husband treats her like a piece of furniture, indifferent that she even exists, I see how her soul is dying. It is impossible to bring this back to life, and if she doesn't make some changes to take care of herself, to find her worth, to create a life that she decides is worth living, I fear the pile of dust she is becoming will be swept away by the next breeze.

In this diagram, conflict is overtaking the relationship. The tension and the honeymoon stages occur less often. Why do you think that is? How do you feel when someone keeps apologizing, but the behavior never changes? How much do the gifts and compliments mean when the person giving them slaps your hand when you reach out to receive them? You likely stop accepting the gifts and compliments. How do you think the person giving gifts and compliments feels when their efforts are being dismissed? You guessed it, a recipe for disaster. Therefore, the relationship is 50 percent conflict.

The Honeymoon stage begins to diminish because the trust in authenticity disappears. The compliments mean less and less, and the gifts make you feel like you are just being bought. It becomes hard to engage when the foundation is crumbling under you.

The Tension stage begins to diminish because it doesn't take much for the aggressor to snap. The habit of just losing control is being created, almost as if it becomes normal to fly off the handle. When the response to tension is consistently abusive, the habit is reinforced. Now, the victim knows it is inevitable and walks on eggshells in anticipation. The person who takes the aggressive role becomes more aggressive, and the person taking the passive role becomes more passive. Both people are getting comfortable in the cycle. Remember, comfortable doesn't always mean healthy.

In Pam's case, she doesn't even try to problem-solve with her husband anymore because it will either turn into insults, disregard, or an argument. They become even more disconnected, and the idea of building intimacy is completely nonexistent. Pam came to me for therapy because she recognized she was becoming a shell of a person and wanted to find her confidence. Validating the toxic cycle of conflict, of which she is a part, was the first step to validating her thoughts and feelings. She is working on setting limits and boundaries with her husband, increasing her social circle outside of the marriage, and shifting her internal dialogue to be supportive and encouraging toward herself. At some point, she may be ready to reevaluate her relationship and determine its course. For now, she has to find herself.

MODULE 5-
CYCLE OF TOXIC
CONFLICT

Honeymoon

Tension

Conflict

"And that's why we stay longer than we should... because it hurts to watch something you love transform into something you should hate. We sit and wait for it to return to its original state, in denial, as we ignore the fact that what we see was always there and what is now, will always be."

—R.H. Sin

In this diagram, you see that the conflict has completely overtaken the relationship. The tension is no longer about the day-to-day stresses. It becomes more about the anxiety. The anxiety of the passive person begins to drive the conflict.

I have another client—I'll call her Beth—in this phase of her relationship. Beth and her husband have been married for seven years. He has a daughter from his previous relationship. It is unclear why that marriage dissolved, but Beth has indicated that the ex-wife was "crazy." I assume these are direct words from Beth's husband. When I met Beth three years ago, she came to therapy to deal with her anxiety, and I've seen her on and off over the years. When she talks about her home life and her marriage, there are many blazing red flags from my perspective. When you are embedded in a relationship like this, it's difficult to see exactly how toxic it is, but from an outsider looking in, it was obvious.

Beth's husband manipulates her to have sex with him daily, sometimes multiple times in a day. He tells her that if she won't have sex, he'll find it elsewhere. Her husband also has a drug addiction, which she stumbled upon while doing laundry and found his drug paraphernalia. This was a shocker to Beth. I had the opportunity to meet her husband because he came to one session with her. I tend to be upfront and direct with my clients because beating around the bush isn't beneficial to anyone, so I gently confronted him with the concerns I saw in the relationship.

We talked about the dance that they had created, each person being responsible for the problematic issues in the relationship. He was not interested in owning any of his actions, he justified his behavior, and he refused to return to therapy. Beth continued therapy for a few more sessions but decided to take a break. Only recently, Beth reached out to me again. She and her husband now have an infant. Beth has learned that her husband is having an affair, he is still doing drugs, and his anger is insurmountable. He isn't involved with the baby, tells Beth the details about his affair, and justifies it since she wasn't giving him sex. He seems to have bouts of guilt, comes crying to her, expresses suicidal ideation, but then flies into a rage. Refusing any mental health assistance, he isn't interested in changing. She finally has packed her belongings and taken her son to live elsewhere until she can sort out her situation.

This is an example of what the diagram looks like where conflict is 80 percent of the relationship, and Honeymoon and tension are only 10 percent. Beth has become so anxiety-ridden in anticipation of her husband eventually getting mad. She knows the aggression and abusive behavior is right around the corner, and instead of waiting for it, she brings up an issue that will set him off, just to hurry up and relieve the tension. She has gotten used to conflict, knows her role in her relationship, and has become so used to the toxic cycle. She is perfecting her part of the dance they have created and instigates the aggressive behavior.

Once these patterns have been established, it is unlikely the couple can pull themselves out of it on their own. This is a common aspect of domestic violence. Within this type of relationship, it is common for the victim to be secretive about what is happening in their lives. They are shameful and embarrassed or feel too stuck and afraid to reach out for help. The aggressor is also stuck in the pattern and won't reach out for help, either because they have blamed their partner for their own behavior for so long that they are blind to the fact that they have an issue or because, like the victim, they feel shame or embarrassment.

When a relationship reaches this last stage, there may well be police involvement and legal ramifications requiring a third party to intervene. If the victim is willing to open up to someone, they may receive enough validation that the situation they are in is extremely abusive and may then reach out for professional help. There they can receive education and counseling to gain the courage to change their situation.

Here you have learned about the cycles of Healthy Conflict and the stages of the cycles of Toxic Conflict.

THE FROG IN THE POT

I'm going to tell you a story about two frogs. I use the story of The Frog in the Pot with clients that I work with. It's really a gross story, and of course, I would never suggest trying this; it is only meant as a visual to make my point. Visualize two pots. One pot contains boiling water. If you throw a frog into the water, it will jump right out because it doesn't want to get cooked. It immediately senses danger, feels the heat, and makes the decision to leap out.

This would be true in a relationship also. If you saw a profile on a dating site of a person saying, "I'm abusive and will wear down your confidence within a month. I'll blame you for behaviors that aren't yours, and I will gaslight you. I will also apologize and give you gifts, but it won't last because I lack coping mechanisms and the desire to change. I am seeking a partner who will allow me to act this way, make excuses for me, and stay with me forever," Would you immediately say, "Sign me up!"? Of course, you wouldn't. You would jump out of that pot faster than lightning.

Second visual. Take a pot of cold water. Place a frog in the cold water and it may swim around for a bit, getting comfortable in its new pot. As you turn the heat on, the frog may get a little uncomfortable, but it adjusts. Continue turning the heat up. The frog changes the places it sits in the pot and continues to adjust, unhappily, but it adjusts. If you continue to turn the heat up, the frog cooks.

In the relationship, the victim is the frog. The victim becomes desensitized to the degrading, abusive behavior they are subjected to, and without realizing, they succumb to the detriment of the relationship.

Don't be the frog in the pot. It is never too late to seek help, to educate yourself. Talk with people who support you, get a therapist. This cycle will not typically change by itself. Honor who you are and be with people who honor you as well. Find your strength and become empowered. You can do this. You are not alone.

THE NEW ME

I know that frog in the second pot. I can pretty much guarantee that an abusive relationship does not fix itself; it is a process of consistently worsening. The heat gets turned up, the heat gets turned down, but every time it turns up, it gets a little bit hotter. I finally had enough influence from family and friends that the relationship I was in had taken such a toll on me that I was unrecognizable. My drive, my confidence, my sparkle was gone. I agreed to get into therapy and move back to my hometown. So, I packed up my two dogs, three cats, all my belongings, and I left. Taking space away, I was able to realize what a fog I'd been in, unable to see the clear picture. I was then able to understand what an abusive relationship is. Emotional and verbal abuse are sometimes more damaging than physical. It's just that the wounds are invisible and therefore harder to acknowledge. Once I was able work through the trauma, get clarity on red flags and personality disorders, I vowed to never get myself caught up in that again. I guarantee you, once you do the work on yourself, any flavor of those abusive behaviors will hit you in the face like a freight train. You will recognize them immediately, not justify them, and jump out of that pot.

SELF-REFLECTION

> "Dear you, make peace with the mirror
> and watch your reflection change."
>
> **—Nina Brown**

Time to get your journal and start reflecting. Here are some questions to answer for yourself.

- With whom are you able to have healthy conflict?
- What is it about them that allows you to feel heard or listened to?
- What makes it possible for you to put your opinions aside and listen to them?
- How did the relationship deepen when you followed the cycle of healthy conflict?
- With whom do you have toxic conflict?
- What are the unresolved issues with this person?
- Within the toxic conflict, with which diagram do you identify?
- What is your part in perpetuating this negative cycle?
- What control do you have over yourself in this relationship, and what can you do to feel more in control?

Remember, you can only control and change yourself. You cannot control or change other people.

CHAPTER 6:
Be Confident and Trust Your Intuition

YOU'RE SINGLE. IT'S FRIDAY night after a long, hectic week, and all you want to do is throw on your yoga pants and binge Netflix. Your girlfriends finally convince you to get out of your yoga pants and into something with a little more "I'm a hottie" flavor because it's time to get back out there, into the jungle. The whole time you are putting on makeup and curling your hair, you tell yourself how ridiculous this idea is and how no one is going to find you halfway attractive. You tell yourself that you'll never be able to carry on an intelligent conversation. Then you seal the deal in your head with the belief that because you've never had a successful relationship, what's the difference now? This mindset has been consistent ever since that last breakup. Whew, that one was a doozy.

Well, aren't you are a boatload of radiating confidence! What happened to you?

Every book, every gimmick, every podcast reference talks of concepts of self-esteem or self-worth. But how do you break this down into something realistic that you can strengthen? It's more than putting the rose-colored glasses on along with your favorite song and hoping everything will turn out okay.

We didn't come out of the womb doubting ourselves and comparing ourselves to other people. This is a learned behavior that, as adults, most of us have perfected. I think the fact that it's a learned behavior is fantastic because that means you can unlearn it, and guess who has 100 percent control over that? You. You don't have to depend on anyone else to make you feel you have worth. You can do this all by yourself, which is a very empowering thought. Remember my mantra: "there is a *why* behind every behavior." So you have to understand the reason behind that lack of confidence. I am going to break down the concept of self-confidence and help you find your starting place on how to ingrain a strong sense of self that will become a new way of life for you.

In this chapter, you will understand why self-confidence and self-respect must be strengthened to have a healthy, loving relationship. If one partner lacks self-worth, think of the destructive patterns that will be formed: jealousy, distrust, manipulation, miscommunication. To be whole and grounded within, you will need to learn forgiveness and the ability to let go of things that no longer serve you. They are crucial to improving your sense of worth.

THE ORIGINATION OF SELF-CONFIDENCE

Chapters 1–5 have taught you how your sense of self was being shaped during those incredibly formative years when you were a child. The concepts of Family Roles, Attachment Styles, communicating our needs, and Conflict Management are important factors that create either a positive or negative sense of self. By about middle school, our beliefs about who we are, are developed. During this stage of life, we begin to use the external factors to reinforce what we have taught ourselves to believe. These experiences of seventh and eighth grade, a time no one ever wants to repeat, further ingrain our concept of self-worth. We ask ourselves questions like, "Am I loveable? Am I a good friend? Am I smart? Will someone ever ask me to dance?" We learn to form an opinion of what we think would make us happy. We compare ourselves to the girls who get picked first in kickball, the couple holding hands as they walk to science class, and the table full of laughing kids in the cafeteria. We wonder, "Do I fit in anywhere?"

By the time high school rolls around, we bring along this persona that we created. There are many forks in the road and degrees of how we can easily be influenced and fall prey to engage in behaviors we aren't psychologically prepared to handle. Developmentally, a teenager's brain isn't prepared to handle the complex ramifications of the damage drugs and alcohol can do or how having sex completely changes a relationship. The brain hasn't developed enough to understand the consequences of impulsive behavior. In fact, the two parts of the brain that are in charge of executive functioning are the frontal lobe and the parietal cortex, which aren't even completely developed until the early twenties. These areas are responsible for planning, reasoning, and focusing. Imagine the choices you made as a teenager. How did these choices affect your confidence? Depending on the choices we make, our peers define what cliques we fall into, which further ingrains our sense of self. What choices do you remember making as a teenager that completely changed the course of your life? How did it affect your concept of self-worth? What events occurred that shaped how you feel about yourself? This degree of confidence will define the upcoming course of your career, your social circle, your finances, and your relationships.

Let's look at ways a negative self-worth can influence a variety of paths you may take in your life, especially as you are seeking a healthy, romantic relationship.

BODY IMAGE AND SELF-CONFIDENCE

I talk with many of my women clients about the perception they have of their bodies. Unfortunately, our society has programmed women, starting at an alarmingly young age, to have unrealistic expectations about how they look. We focus on parts of our bodies that are "imperfect" and are taught to despise these parts, and most of us go to unhealthy lengths to try and fix whatever we think is wrong and meet society's standards.

For example, how often do you stand naked in the mirror, admiring your body with loving-kindness? Did you just laugh out loud and spit out your wine? Well, grab a napkin and wipe your face. No, we sit in front of a mirror, with or without clothes on, and curse at ourselves, poking, pinching, crying about everything we hate about our image. When we finally wipe the tears and walk away, where is our level of confidence? In the toilet. Negative body image is just one aspect that influences our confidence, but you can imagine how it infiltrates so many aspects of our lives.

A lack of confidence leads us to have a distorted perception of our surroundings. When I am working with clients to help improve confidence, I use a cognitive behavioral approach. This form of therapy means that by changing your thinking, you can change your behavior. David Burns and Aaron Beck are the founding fathers of Cognitive Behavioral Therapy, and I credit them when I use the *Distorted Thinking* list. This includes ten ways we can distort our perception just by allowing our minds to go unchecked. Becoming aware of your thought process is the first step to changing what isn't working. Shifting the unproductive ways of thinking is the second step.

For this example, I will use the concept of negative body image and apply it to these ten distorted ways of thinking. I will show you the destructive way of thinking and then shift it into a constructive way of thinking. As you read the examples, reflect on your own patterns of thought. Identify ways you get caught up in this mind storm. You can't change something if you aren't aware of it, so this is your first step.

- All or Nothing
  - o Destructive: I can never stick to a diet, and I'll always be fat.
  - o Constructive: Eating healthier makes me feel better, and I'm valuable whether I'm thin or not.

- Overgeneralization
  - Destructive: I missed a day on the treadmill. I am such a failure.
  - Constructive: Tomorrow is a new day, and I will dedicate time to exercise.

- Mental Filter
  - Destructive: I am an ugly person because I have a muffin top.
  - Constructive: I am proud of who I am as a person. I have gorgeous eyes and a loving heart.

- Discounting Positives
  - Destructive: My partner says I am beautiful, but he is obviously delusional.
  - Constructive: I appreciate my partner's compliments.

- Mind Reading/Fortune Telling
  - Destructive: Walking on the beach causes me so much anxiety because I know everyone is looking and making fun of my skinny, spaghetti legs.
  - Constructive: Who cares if anyone is looking at me? I'm having a nice time no matter what anyone thinks. It's nobody's business how I look.

- Jumping to Conclusions
  - Destructive: I know I will never find love. Who could ever love me the way I look?

- Constructive: When I can learn to love myself, I can be available for a healthy, loving relationship.

- Emotional Reasoning
  - Destructive: I feel like my partner is disgusted by my body, so it must be true.
  - Constructive: I can ask my partner how he feels about my body, and then I must trust his words.

- "Should" Statements
  - Destructive: I shouldn't be so lazy and just go work out.
  - Constructive: I will create an exercise plan that works with my schedule and dedicate time to make it happen.

- Labeling
  - Destructive: Ugh, I am a fat piece of shit.
  - Constructive: I am lovable and deserve happiness and internal peace.

- Blaming
  - Destructive: If people didn't take up so much of my time, I could work out, and then I would be happier with my body.
  - Constructive: I am in control of my schedule, and I make time for what is important to me.

If you just now had the realization that you participate in a few of these destructive ways of thinking, join the club. It is very common to get caught up in this trap. These types of statements can set you and/or other people up to fail. They can cause you to miss out on some great opportunities in life. How can you have confidence in yourself or other people when this is the thought process? Pick one of the distorted ways of thinking that you use the most. Now catch yourself when you do this and really challenge yourself to shift it into a constructive way of talking to yourself.

WHO ARE YOU UNDER THAT LAYER OF PROTECTION?

A lack of confidence also keeps us from being our genuine, authentic selves in a relationship. Not trusting your intuition makes you second-guess your thoughts and feelings. You can hold back what you want to say or how you say things. This can keep people at a distance or keep them from understanding your intentions. I have a client I'll call Lori, who is a gorgeous, intelligent accountant. In her professional life, she has been very successful, owning her own business and maintaining a steady flow of clients. However, in her personal life, her confidence is in the toilet. She can't maintain a romantic relationship because she either pushes men away or won't engage with them at all for fear of rejection. She has become so shy that people create a perception that she is stuck-up and entitled. Now, she has a difficult time even making new friends because of her unapproachable nature. These factors reinforce her lack of confidence. My first impression when I saw Lori in my waiting room for the first time was that she likely had a thriving social life and a satisfying romantic relationship. I never would have guessed she had an issue with confidence. This goes to show that you never know another person's internal struggles. Lori is working on gaining awareness of her thoughts and either connecting them with a realistic, fact-based situation and taking control over the outcome or determining that her thoughts are not fact-based and recognizing when she is creating a negative, fantasy-based story. If her thoughts are based on reality—for example, "I haven't been able to maintain a loving relationship"—this is true because she hasn't been able to do this. Lori's goal is to understand why this is and what she has control over in order to change this. She is developing ways to deal with that situation, work through it, and find a lesson to learn. If it is based in fantasy—for example, "Everyone hates me and thinks I'm worthless"—this is not fact-based. No one has ever actually said this to Lori, so now she has an opportunity to recognize her fantasy thought process and challenge it. In therapy, Lori is recognizing that she's creating the negativity in her mind and is working to shift it to a more positive, empowering thought. Changes like these take time and require patience.

Low self-confidence also leads to being defensive and guarded. I have another client I will call Joe who came to therapy because he kept getting passed up on promotions at work. His boss said it was because Joe was angry and didn't engage with his colleagues and that if Joe wanted to become a manager, he had to develop positive, working relationships with people. But Joe had a hard time trusting people and assumed they were judging or out to get him. He lacked the internal confidence and used his armor to protect his fragile ego. Joe would not allow himself to show any vulnerability in the workplace. He also shared with me that his romantic relationship was beginning to suffer. Because Joe was not being promoted, he assumed he wasn't capable of performing well at work. If he couldn't do his job, Joe thought he must be a horrible person and started to believe his wife probably thought he was a horrible husband. That thought led him to believe he didn't deserve such a loving partner. Irritated and angry, he began to distance himself from her. You can see the snowball effect in action here.

If you want to have healthy relationships with others, you need vulnerability. Having boundaries and setting limits is important, but to relate to and connect with people, you must let down your guard, and this requires a degree of healthy confidence.

INTERNAL AND EXTERNAL FACTORS

Do you rely on internal or external factors to make you feel confident? Take my client, "Alex," a young adult, age twenty. She lives at home after taking an early leave from college a few years ago. Alex was a straight-A student through high school. Her confidence came from people telling her how smart she was. She'd fly through her classes with the greatest of ease, and her confidence grew with every positive comment from teachers. Alex experimented with a variety of classes, stretching outside of her comfort zone. Continuing to excel, she felt reassurance through others that she was intelligent. In college, she was challenged in her classes, quickly learning the monumental difference from what she was used to. As she sat in the stadium seats, her professors looked like tiny specs pacing across the floor, speaking through a microphone. They would likely never know who she was, let alone give her any positive reinforcement. The first sign of struggle occurred in statistics, then chemistry, and soon she was doubting her intelligence in all her classes. As Alex's grades plummeted, along with her confidence, her anxiety catapulted.

Alex had defined herself based on what people thought about her intelligence, and she had never relied on her internal sense of confidence. Without others giving her glowing feedback, she no longer believed she could pass college courses. The anxiety led to depression, which resulted in Alex leaving college and moving back home after her first year. Her family and friends were shocked, and Alex was mortified. She relied solely on external factors to give her a temporary sense of confidence. When the validation from others that made her feel confident was no longer available, she realized she never believed in herself. Her goal in therapy is to strengthen her internal dialogue and prove to herself she is capable of setting and achieving goals.

Relying on only external validation both holds you back and keeps you stuck. I have worked with another young adult I'll call Tim. He grew up a star soccer athlete, the external factor. Everyone always told him how great he was because he scored the most points, ran the fastest, blocked the best, and shuffled the ball with utmost talent. He received amazing validation for being wonderful because of his soccer abilities. It came easy to him, and he was the most confident out on the field. His sense of self was based on his amazing soccer talents but not on any other character attributes.

After college soccer, he burned out and no longer wanted to play competitive soccer. Tim told me about a time his friends invited him to go golf. He'd never golfed but figured he was an athlete, so he was confident, and he'd get out there and show them a thing or two. Well, he quickly learned that he was horrible at golf, not because he didn't have the ability, but because he'd never played before. His ball went in the water, into the trees, sliced to the right, and hooked to the left. He decided he'd never play golf again. This became a pattern for Tim. If something didn't come easily, he quit. If he wasn't perfect at a task, he gave up. The more scenarios he was faced with, the more he convinced himself he would fail, and his confidence tanked. The minute Tim wasn't the best at something, his fear of failure kept him from getting out of his comfort zone and trying new things. He held back from taking risks, such as interviewing for jobs or asking women on dates. The lack of confidence turned into anxiety, and Tim became an empty shell. His goals in therapy are to build a strong internal sense of self and learn to take calculated risks. By setting short-term, realistic goals, Tim will build his confidence and learn to laugh at his mistakes while offering positive reinforcement to his successes.

Of course, external validation feels great, and we all love it when it happens, but it is risky to rely on that to make you feel good about yourself. Internal validation is what provides stability, while external validation should be a bonus and not something we look to complete us.

BOUNDARIES

What are boundaries, and why are they crucial to your confidence? Boundaries are the limits you set with other people and how you communicate to others what behavior you find acceptable and unacceptable. Setting healthy boundaries with others requires a strong level of confidence. When you compromise this, you also compromise yourself. When you think of what boundaries look like, you most likely think of the physical type—the actual space you create between you and another person. However, boundaries are important to maintain in other areas too.

Mental boundaries are knowing what you want and what you think and not letting others twist your thoughts. Sexual boundaries are being able to ask for what you want and say what you don't want, as well as consent or refusing sex. Verbal boundaries include speaking with respect and not letting others be verbally abusive toward you. Monetary boundaries are about not going into unrecoverable debt or allowing someone to take advantage of your finances. Time boundaries are not being late or not allowing others to take advantage of your time. Time boundaries also include not putting too many items on your to-do list so that you have no time to complete what you need to and become overly stressed. Spiritual boundaries are freely believing what you want to and not being brainwashed or pressured to believe differently.

Having weak or loose boundaries means you are not respecting what is important to you. Have you ever defined what you want your boundaries to look like?

Using the categories of physical, mental, verbal, monetary, time, and spirituality, I encourage you to write out what this would look like if you were honoring yourself by creating and maintaining these healthy limits. These are boundaries you set with yourself as well as what you require from other people. When you demonstrate healthy boundaries, you leave zero room for others to violate you, therefore, requiring them to respect you too.

When your boundaries get compromised, you will feel a sense of negativity in your body. Your body is always talking to you. Think about this. When you are starving, what is your stomach doing? Yes, growling. How about when you're freezing cold? What is your body doing? Yes, shivering. All right, how about when you are exhausted. What happens? You got it. You yawn, and your eyes water. Can you voluntarily make these things happen? No, you cannot. When you beg for that crystal ball, hoping to know what you need to feel happy and content, your body is already screaming its needs to you. The hard part is to pay attention. If you don't see the small signs, your body will keep yelling and increasing the red flags. Pretty soon, you will feel anxiety or panic attacks, high blood pressure, disease, etc. You get the picture. So, when you compromise your boundaries, your body will let you know. Strong, healthy confidence equals strong, healthy boundaries.

PERSONALIZING

When your confidence is compromised, it is easy to fall into the common trap of personalization. Personalization is assuming responsibility for someone else's behavior. When this occurs, a whirlwind of negative outcomes will follow. Assumptions, pressure, lack of accountability, miscommunication, and loss of self-worth are a few of these outcomes. Not only do they take a personal toll, but they also affect your relationships with other people.

Here you are, walking down the hallway at work. You pass a colleague and say hello. No response. Immediately, your mind starts recalling past events, and you start wondering why they are mad at you. Did you say something offensive in an email? Did you disappoint them and didn't know it? Oops, you just personalized. The stories you create in your head about what the other person was feeling have you irritated and wondering what happened. The next time you see that colleague, you may act cold and flippant. Why? Because you personalized something and have zero facts to back it up.

I have a client I will call Teri who came to counseling because she has anxiety and feels lonely and isolated. She hasn't been able to maintain a romantic relationship longer than about eight months. In dissecting Teri's situation, we pinpointed her major downfall—personalization. Teri dated a guy I'll call Ray. Things were going along pretty well the first few months they were dating. Based on Teri's track record, she started getting nervous that the relationship wouldn't last, and her confidence was tested. She started picking up on some of Ray's behaviors and made them more about her without checking it out with Ray. For example, Teri would text Ray, and he wouldn't get back to her for a few hours. She would ask him to plan a trip with her, and he wouldn't show the same enthusiasm as she did. These smaller behaviors became more and more apparent to Teri. She figured Ray was distancing himself, not wanting to talk with her, not wanting to make future plans because he had no intention of creating a lasting relationship with her. She began getting frustrated when he would finally return her texts.

He, on the other hand, had no idea what was happening because he felt content and happy with Teri. When he pointed out her tone of frustration, Teri became angrier with him because she felt he was blaming her and acting irrationally. Not only could Ray not speak to her about how he felt, but he had no idea what had shifted between them.

Here is a great example of how personalizing other people's behavior leads to the creation of a fictional story in your head and how easy it is to act on that story. Once Teri finally communicated to Ray about how she was feeling, he had the opportunity to tell her he was swamped at work and fearful of losing his job because of cutbacks. He was afraid to plan a trip together because of financial issues. His behavior had nothing to do with Teri.

In this situation, Ray may start to feel he can't voice his concerns because of Teri's anger. He might not have felt he had the opportunity to tell her his side of the story because she had convinced herself he didn't want to be with her anymore. When one partner personalizes behaviors that aren't theirs, the other person has a difficult time trying to understand what went wrong. Why? First, they have no idea what to even explain because they don't know why their partner is angry. Second, when they do try to explain, it's almost too late, and they don't have a chance. The defensive wall their partner has thrown up makes effective communication impossible. Any constructive criticism that Ray may have had for Teri was filtered through the story she had fabricated, and his perspective was left unheard. Because of Teri's insecurities, the things Ray says will only reinforce her negative dialogue, and she will continue to react with anger. When personalization gets left unattended, conflict and insecurities build, tearing a relationship apart.

COMPARING YOURSELF TO OTHERS

We are taught to compare from a young age. That boy got the lead role in the play because he was better at memorizing lines. That girl got picked to be the captain of the volleyball team because she was the best player. As an adult, you compare things all the time. "Do I wear a coat today? It's colder today than it was yesterday, so comparing temperatures, yes, I will wear a coat." "Am I successful? I don't know," you ask, "compared to what?" Asking yourself comparing type questions like these is completely normal. It helps you gauge whether to be satisfied or if you need to change your situation to become more satisfied. However, when comparing becomes unhealthy, it is because the intention behind the comparison was based on insecurities and fears.

Social media is a wonderful tool that offers the ability to connect with people you never would have gotten the chance to know. It allows us to follow famous people, hear others' opinions, and stay up to date on the latest and greatest, well, everything. But used in the wrong way, social media can be a detriment. If you are already struggling with confidence and your insecurities are high, social media is the last place to spend a lot of time browsing around. When you are in this emotional state, you are more likely to compare yourself to everyone you see. You are more likely to compare up, feeling less than.

Are you aware of how often you compare yourself to other people and feel like you are failing or not good enough? Again, I think we are groomed to do this at a young age. Commercials tell us that we aren't thin enough, so we need a diet product. They tell us we are not naturally beautiful and need ten pounds of makeup. They tell us we are not aging gracefully and need snips, tucks, and surgery. As a teenager, I cut out the pages of models in *Seventeen* magazine and hung them on my bedroom wall. I would study these women, their smooth, cellulite-free skin, how they sat, what they wore, who they talked to. I would strive to be just like them, but when glancing in the mirror, I was short and curvy. Plus, I couldn't put a fashionable outfit together to save my life. Big fail. It's no different today, only now, the pictures are right there on your phone, and you can see one hundred people in five minutes versus eight models in that monthly magazine. We are inundated with people, places, relationships, homes, jobs, cars, and more to compare ourselves to. Are you in the trap? I have a solution.

There are parts of yourself that are never going to change, ever. Then there are parts of yourself that can be adjusted. I always thought it would be amazing to be five-seven. You could reach things on the top shelves at the store, you could see over people sitting in front of you at the movies, you could see the stage at a concert. But I have been five-three-and-a-half for as long as I can remember. This is something that will never change. In fact, it will likely go the other direction in the coming years. However, here is an example that I do have control over. I tend to be a pile person: I have stacks of papers, books, folders, nick-knacks, and stuff. I would like to simplify and get more organized. Is this something I can change? You bet.

What does this have to do with comparing yourself to other people? Well, here is your task:

- First, become aware of when you compare yourself to someone else. Are you feeling empowered or depleted by this comparison? Observe these negative thoughts.

- Second, evaluate if there is truth to these thoughts. Are you really a failure because that person has a great job and makes a ton of money? Maybe you actually like your job. Maybe you decide that if you didn't spend frivolously, you wouldn't be in debt. When you really step back, you wouldn't want that person's job because they have zero free time and work seventy-plus-hour weeks. You wish them well, and then you let the thought go.

- However, if you become aware of the comparison to the person with the fabulous job and reflect on your current position, deciding you're a failure, you have some options. Accept that you hate your job, or figure out some short-term, realistic goals to make a change. Short-term, because you need some immediate gratification. Realistic, because you don't want to set yourself up for failure.

- As you start with the first step to make a change in your job structure, you give yourself credit and keep going. As you make progress, you realize you are in control of your life, and your confidence begins to build. See what happened? You shifted from feeling like a failure to taking action to change something you didn't like.

MODULE 5-
SELF-CONFIDENCE

 **What I like about me:**

⊖ **What I don't like about me:**

▶ Do I have a positive/negative internal sense of self? Why?

▶ Do I rely on my external sense of self? Why?

▶ Do I seek attention or avoid attention? Why?

▶ Do I seek approval from others? Why? From whom?

▶ Do I compare myself to others? Who?

In this diagram, you have an opportunity to identify what you like about yourself and what you do not like. Answering the questions will allow you to evaluate aspects of yourself that are directly related to confidence. Apply the distorted thinking examples and commit to making changes in your life that only lead to self-acceptance. You are ultimately the only person who can change the degree of confidence. Where will you start? Where will you focus your attention and energy?

SELF-REFLECTION

There are many ways to develop and strengthen confidence. I've given you a few ideas in this chapter, but here are a few more:

- Develop a coping statement. This is a one-liner, a simple sentence that you say to yourself one hundred times a day for two weeks straight. Say it as you're driving, while you're in the shower, while you're walking through the grocery store. The more you say it to yourself and out loud, the more ingrained it will become. You won't believe it at first, and that's the point. But over time, you will begin to find its truth, and it will become a way of life. The one I used and still use was one I started more than fifteen years ago. It is, "I don't have to prove myself to anyone." When I am in a situation where I feel intimidated, it pops into my mind and rolls right off my tongue. I have practiced this mantra for so many years that it is now ingrained and a part of my soul. What is your mantra? A few to choose from are:

- o I am worthy of being loved.
- o I deserve to be happy.
- o I am successful and satisfied in my life.
- o I can be calm and in control of myself.

- Make a list of things you are grateful for before you go to bed. This may help you change your focus and give you something to look for throughout the day.

- Pay it forward. Doing kind things for others gets you out of your head. Knowing you are positively impacting someone else's life immediately makes you feel better.

FINDING FORGIVENESS

Can you think of what forgiveness has to do with confidence? Why do you think it's important to forgive? Why would forgiving others for things that happened in the past and forgiving yourself for mistakes you've made help you feel more empowered?

The idea here is to acknowledge the issues in the past that continue to surface, which cause you pain, cause you to replay conversations, feelings, reactions, and events. Hitting the rewind and play button does nothing for your confidence because you can't forget what happened, you can't change it, and you can't do anything about it. The past is set in stone. Replaying and worrying about it only causes grief, anxiety, and heartache. You have to identify it, work through it, find forgiveness and let it go, which leads to finding peace.

MODULE 5-
FORGIVENESS

Acknowledge

Work it out

Find forgiveness

Let it go

First, I think it is important to define forgiveness. Forgiving someone or ourselves doesn't mean that what happened was alright. You may think back to events and traumas you endured and think something like, *There is no way I can forgive that!* While it is always wrong to harm someone, be mean, or cause pain, forgiveness is more about you being able to find peace with a situation. What is it that you need to do so that every time you think of that particular situation, your blood pressure doesn't go through the roof, and you don't get so angry that the rest of your day is ruined?

I suggest you take a few minutes to think back on your life of the events that continue to surface and cause you internal pain and struggle. These will be marked as points necessary to find forgiveness. Where would you even start to do this exercise? Begin with a timeline. Draw a horizontal line on a sheet of unlined paper. On the left-hand side is the earliest memory you have of an event that caused you heartache. The right-hand side of the line marks today. For example, the first time I really experienced emotional pain was when I was about seven or eight years old. I was in gymnastics and dance, and one of my friends made fun of my teeth. (I was a thumb sucker, what can I say?) That makes me think of a time at this camp in sixth grade, and a boy said I wasn't invited to the dance because only the pretty girls could go. Oh, now I'm on a roll. I start writing down all kinds of things up until today that have happened and scarred my soul.

As you remember these events, try to take a few minutes and allow your mind to recall your own events that caused pain, sorrow, trauma, confusion, mistreatment, disappointment. Whether you caused these emotions or outcomes, or

someone else did, write the memories down. You can categorize the experiences by the grade you were in, by seasons,
and by places you lived. This might make recalling the
events a little easier.

I would suggest spending only about eight minutes on
this timeline. I'm an eight-minute girl. Five doesn't seem to
be enough, and ten is too long. You'd be surprised how much
can be recalled once you start peeling that onion of memories. Also, I don't want you spending too much time recalling
events because, one, it can be overwhelming, and two, I
want you to spend more time working toward letting these
memories go. If you have too much anxiety while recalling
events, put down your pen, take some deep breaths, and
when you are ready, come back to the exercise. Make sure
you come back because this is the part that helps anxiety
and enhances confidence.

Once you have identified the key incidents that you
have held onto, think about what you need to do to feel the
emotions, to be able to sit with the unsettling feeling. Maybe
you identify what that feeling is. Is it loss, fear, shock, disappointment, rejection, abandonment? Was this something
that you caused? Do you need to own your behavior? Is this
something that someone did to you? Who was it? What did
that relationship mean to you? Take some time to answer
these questions.

The final question to answer can be the most infor-
mative and healing in the forgiveness process. What could
have been going on with them that they treated you this
way? Or, if you are the perpetrator, what was going on with
you that you caused this unfortunate event? When finding
forgiveness, this last question requires some deep thinking.

You know my mantra: there is always a *why*, a reason for every single behavior. Rarely does someone just walk up to another person and punch them in the face or call them a name. There are emotions behind this behavior. Again, it does not excuse the behavior, but it can help create space between you and the actual action (not personalizing other people's stuff), and it helps create a sense of compassion.

The first house I ever bought was in Denver in an area that I now wouldn't even drive through at two in the afternoon. I moved in, and it didn't take long before I began to feel unsafe. Gunshots, yelling, and sirens were the common nighttime noises. One day, a kind neighbor told me that the kids who lived on the other side of my house were shooting bb's at my two dogs while I was at work. I was enraged. Other horrible behaviors I experienced, which I'm certain were the boys next door, were coming home to find used condoms on my doorstep and urine on my door handle. Disgusting, right? After confronting the lady who owned the house, I learned that she was the grandmother of the kids who lived there. The mother was in jail for heroin possession and whatever else, and the father wasn't around and hadn't been for quite some time. She was trying to raise the adolescent boys on her own and felt very out of control. I spoke to the boys, who probably couldn't have cared less about me, my dogs, or my home, but at least I confronted them. When I moved, I gave the grandmother and the boys a ton of items I no longer needed. The look of gratitude and surprise on their faces was priceless. One of the boys asked why I would do this when they had been so nasty. I can't remember what I said or any other exchanges, but this is an example of finding forgiveness. I felt a level of compassion for these boys. They had lost their mother and father. Who knows what kind of trauma they had been through as small children? They were angry, acting out, but I know that just under the layer of anger, there is always fear. I had a choice to continue to be angry and let my blood pressure go up and feel a sense of rage, which eventually would only be expressed on the people closest to me, or I could try to dig for a sense of compassion and act from that. One way will kill me; the other way allows me to acknowledge it, feel it, find forgiveness, and let it go.

I encourage you to try to do the same. Go back to your timeline. Answer the questions, and please be patient with yourself. Are you ready to find forgiveness and release the emotionally consuming grip it holds on you?

There is a time for forgiveness and a time to take personal safety measures. Important side note here. Be aware that if someone is treating you badly repeatedly, this forgiveness process does not mean that you have to continuously be a punching bag for that person. For instance, I forgave the boys next door to me and showed them kindness, but I also maintained my self-respect by moving. If you are currently in an abusive situation, evaluate the following:

- Are you in a dangerous situation that you need to leave and seek self-protection?

- Is the person with whom you are involved owning or taking any responsibility for their actions? If not, I guarantee you, they are not going to change.

- Do you need to own or take responsibility for your own actions in order to change?

If you are safe, then doing the timeline and using the communication and conflict resolution skills you have learned in the previous chapters may help you work toward forgiveness and letting go.

There are lessons to be learned in any situation. If you look back and realize you were to blame for causing a chaotic event, the goal is about understanding why and what you need to do to change your ways. When you can identify and implement changes, your confidence improves. As you ingrain the lesson and put it into action, that will soon be the "normal" behavior, making it less likely that you'll slip back into the destructive behavior.

If you look back and need to forgive someone else, the goal is to let go of the past, speak up about what you will no longer tolerate, reevaluate a relationship, or leave the relationship because it is not going to change. Any of these actions result in forwarding progress in your life and will ultimately improve confidence.

SELF-REFLECTION

- Acknowledge the situations from your past that you hold on to and which cause you pain and stress.

- Process the feelings that emerge when looking at these situations.

- Work through the emotional struggle using coping mechanisms or seeking therapy with a professional.

- Find forgiveness. This does not excuse the behavior, but it allows you to find internal peace.

- Let it go. Release the emotional talon from your soul.

Having a strong sense of self and letting go of what no longer serves you will allow you to show up in any relationship, especially a romantic relationship, and be 100 percent available. It will also allow you to accept your partner for who they are instead of treating them like they are everyone who ever hurt you from your past.

Go be free.

CHAPTER 7:
The Cone of Fear: What You're Really Afraid Of

"You do not move ahead by constantly
looking in a rear-view mirror. The past is a
rudder to guide you, not an anchor to drag
you. We must learn from the past but not
live in the past."

—Warren W. Wiersbe

HAVE A FEW BINS filled with memories in my garage. Inside these bins are everything from baby books and my favorite stuffed animals to yearbooks and journal after journal overflowing with the woes of my teenage years. I even found a journal that had seventeen lines beginning with "I Love," followed by the names of boys, one crossed out as another was added. This made me chuckle as I read each name and recalled that "life-ending" heartbreak I'd felt. Shoot, with that many breaks, my heart probably looks like a mirror ball with a million pieces taped together.

I have a frame of my first true love, high school and college graduation caps, my wedding book, and stacks of photos of my kids. In another bin, I also have my divorce paperwork, bills, and taxes. That bin is in the back corner of the garage with the spiders. No matter how far back it is shoved, memories are stacked in that bin too.

Each of us has a past. Good memories, bad memories. Experiences we treasure and those we wish to forget. Relationships that left scars and those we hold close to our hearts. We all have them, and for better or worse, we'll never forget them. Our past is what shapes us into who we are today. It's what gives us the framework for how we feel about ourselves and what influences the choices we make.

But what if we just glide blindly through these experiences? What if we just accept these experiences for what they are, just a space in time? What happens when we don't take the time to dissect them and learn from all they have to offer? Will we just keep repeating our actions? How do we know if how we handled these situations was helpful or destructive? So many questions that, if left unanswered, could be paving the path for continued heartache without us even realizing that we are predicting our destiny!

In this chapter, you will dissect your past relationships. Although these may be romantic, familial, or friend relationships, the goal of this exercise will be to improve your ability to choose a person best suited for a healthy, romantic relationship. All relationships in your past had positive and negative aspects, and I'll guide you to identify all sides of the learning opportunities. By doing this, you will use your past as a tapestry to learn about not only what other people did to contribute to your ups and downs but also how your own behavior led to fulfillment or heartache.

Then, we will look at how the power of fear can control your behavior and reactions to situations. This will help you understand the root cause of many negative behaviors. When this is clear, you'll see you have a choice to personalize other people's behavior or not. It will also help you take control over your reactions because you will learn to react from an understanding of the *why* versus reacting from impulse. By ingraining these concepts, you will learn to promote a healthy relationship and avoid repeating the mistakes of the past.

Finally, you will use all of this information to develop your list of non-negotiables for your relationship. This is a list that, no matter what, you do not deviate from! It is what you believe in, how you value your worth, and how you display the highest level of respect for yourself.

MODULE 6- TIMELINE OF A RELATIONSHIP

|————————————————————————————|

**Earliest
Relationship**

**Most Recent
Relationship**

❖ **What were the positive aspects of each relationship?**

❖ **Why did each relationship end?**

❖ **Why did I stay?**

❖ **What were the red flags?**

❖ **What did I learn?**

❖ **What was my personal responsibility for this relationship?**

DISSECTING THE PAST

Our past relationships offer us information like a three-dimensional topography map. They show us the mountains we had to climb, the valleys we slid down, the crevices we climbed out of. Now you will pick apart your past relationships and learn what lessons they provided.

Use the example in this diagram to draw your own relationship timeline. The left side of your line is the earliest relationship you can remember, and on the right is the most recent or current relationship. Now make vertical lines to note each relationship. Write the names of as many people who impacted your life as you can remember. You may mostly remember romantic relationships, but if there was a mentor or a friendship that marked a turning point in your life, you can write that down too. With each relationship, you can use your journal to expand as you answer the questions that follow. Make a note of when the relationship took place and how long it lasted.

To learn as much as you can about each relationship, I'll guide you through these questions. Spend some time answering each question as it pertains to each relationship.

1. **What were the positive and negative aspects of each relationship?**
   a. There were likely positive aspects in the relationship; otherwise, you wouldn't have stayed. By looking at the positives, you can identify what is important to you. What made you have a close connection with that person? Did you travel, like the same music, have mutual friends? Did you feel

appreciated, respected? Was it easy to be yourself?

b. What were the negative aspects in each relationship? Did you feel heard? Did you feel important? Where did you feel disconnected? Were these negative aspects apparent from the beginning of the relationship, or did they slowly develop over time? Did you feel like you walked on eggshells? Were you able to be your authentic self?

c. Take note of these positive and negative aspects because you will refer to this when we talk about non-negotiables.

2. **Why did each relationship end?**

a. Was it a mutual ending, or was one person wanting to work it out, and the other was done?

b. If you initiated the ending, how long were you unhappy before you actually ended the relationship?

c. When you look back at the relationship, do you have regrets? What are they? What would you have done differently?

d. Do you feel like you drag aspects of this relationship into the relationships that followed? If so, what aspects are these? If you do, it could be demonstrated by treating your next or current partner based on your old partner's behaviors. For example, if your past partner cheated, you could have serious trust issues with the next partner, even though they didn't do anything to deserve the mistrust.

e. Do you need to find forgiveness with your-self or the other person? If so, what aspects do you need to forgive?

f. Have you found closure from this relation-ship that no longer exists?

3. Why did you stay?

a. Did you want out but stayed longer than you should have? Why?

b. Did you go back and forth with the breakups and getting back together? Was there ever a resolution?

c. Were you promised changes by the other person that never happened? Were you promising changes to your partner that you couldn't fulfill?

d. Did the relationship become an obsession? An addiction? You knew it was bad for you, but you kept going back for more?

e. If you are emotionally hanging on to this past relationship, what do you need to do to find closure?

4. What red flags or warning signs can you now clearly see in each relationship?

a. Getting some distance from a relationship helps you to see the dynamics much more clearly. What aspects do you see now that you couldn't see when you were involved in the relationship?

b. Were these red flags apparent at the beginning?

c. Were you aware of these issues but hoped they would go away?

d. How did you compromise yourself based on these issues, and what did that do to your confidence?

e. Did you voice your concern to your partner when the red flags appeared, or did you keep it to yourself or talk with a third party?

f. If so, what was the outcome? If you didn't voice your concerns to your partner, what kept you from speaking up?

5. **What did you learn from each relationship— about yourself and about your partner?**

a. All experiences allow learning opportunities. Each relationship provided eye-opening learning lessons around honoring yourself, setting boundaries, being authentic, resolving conflict, and utilizing healthy communication techniques. Think of these aspects as well as any other aspects that come to mind when answering this question.

b. Take a moment to journal around this section because it is so important to really spend some time and ingrain what is coming to the forefront of your mind.

c. As the lessons become clear, challenge yourself and ask what needs to either change in your current romantic relationship or what you would do differently in your future romantic relationship.

d. By paying attention here, you can assure that you won't repeat mistakes from the past. And if you happen to repeat them, you will be able to recognize right when the mistake occurs and will be able to rectify the situation faster. When you don't recognize a behavior as a mistake, you're likely to keep repeating it. That is why this section is so crucial to developing healthy, romantic relationships.

6. **What was your personal responsibility for this relationship ending?**

Although I believe it always takes two people to make a relationship work and two to make it fall apart, it is always easier to point the finger at the other person to find blame. This question isn't about what the other person did though; this is about taking a hard look in the mirror and identifying what your personal responsibility was in the relationship. Blaming may keep you protected from feeling grief, but that won't help you learn and do things differently going forward. Take a deep breath and know that acknowledgement leads to feeling empowered because you will be able to take control of your life moving forward.

a. What were negative aspects in each relationship that you contributed to? Looking back at topics we have discussed, were you assertive enough? Did you communicate your needs effectively? Did you manage your conflict resolution skills effectively? Did you compromise your non-negotiables? Did you even have a list of non-negotiables?

b. Why do you think you behaved that way? Was it based on a fear of getting hurt, so you acted with defensiveness? Were you out of options and acted from survival? Was it hard to be direct, so you used indirect methods to get your needs met? Understanding why you acted the way you did will help you learn and shift things to make healthier choices going forward.

c. After identifying what your contribution was to why the relationship ended, do you need to seek professional help from a psychotherapist to work through these issues? Maybe you have experienced trauma in your life and require counseling to deal with these issues? Perhaps there is unresolved grief or negativity from your past, and you would benefit from seeking help to develop the skills necessary to allow yourself to move forward to find your internal happiness.

7. **Do you need to find forgiveness?**

As we talked about in the last chapter, finding forgiveness is not about saying a bad behavior was acceptable. It is more about finding peace within. By forgiving, you find your confidence and a way to move forward with compassion and an open heart.

    a. What do you need to forgive?

    b. Whom do you need to forgive?

    c. How will you find this forgiveness? (Feel free to refer back to the previous chapter about forgiveness.)

CONE OF FEAR

Critical
Cold Shoulder
Controlling   Sarcastic
Jealousy Judgemental Angry

DEFENSIVE

DEPRESSION

WORRY

GUILT

SHAME

F E A R

Rejection   Abandonment

THE CONE OF FEAR

Imagine waltzing onto a battleground without any armor, no protection, no power to defend. How long would you last? A nanosecond? Right. Now imagine being in a romantic relationship without a way to communicate, without any boundaries, without an understanding of what you even need to feel loved. How long would you last here? Not long.

Okay, let's add one more component. Let's add on a couple of decades of living life into the mix. Heartache, setbacks, traumas. This isn't to say you haven't had positive occurrences in your life, but love, laughter, and warm fuzzies don't create negative actions. Once again, remember my motto: "there is always a *why* behind every behavior," and here, we will dissect the *why*. What's the purpose of understanding the *why*? A better question is, what is the risk if you don't understand the *why*? When you can pause and not react to the actual behavior, but instead take a step back and take a deep breath, you can separate the emotional reaction from the cause of that emotion. Separate the angry reaction from the reason that caused such a chaotic and panicked response. When you are able to do this, there are a few things that will happen:

1. You won't personalize other people's behavior and actions.

2. You will help to decrease the defensiveness of the other person.

3. If this is Self-reflection, you will gain an understanding of what you need to work on within to
   not impulsively react. This deeper level of realization is the root of the emotion.

In this diagram, you see a cone shape. This is called the
Cone of Fear. At the top of the cone are behaviors that are
expressed outward. Think of lava shooting out of a volcano,
causing chaos. Here we have shutting down, giving the cold
shoulder, and being critical, controlling, sarcastic, jealous,
judgmental, and angry.

What are some other negatively expressed behaviors
you can think of? Write them at the top of the cone. These
are all behaviors that a person feels will protect them. When
you are guarding the vulnerability, you have the idea that it
is easier to be angry than to be sad. However, this protection
is likely to keep you secluded and lonely.

For five years, I conducted court-ordered domestic
violence training classes—one for men and one for women.
The people in my group had been arrested for domestic
violence and were being forced to attend a thirty-six-week
program and pay between twenty-five and forty dollars per
class, based on their income. They likely had to complete a
urinalysis or breathalyzer before each class if drugs or alcohol
were present at the time of arrest. On top of the cost for all of
this, they had to pay a probation officer, and they likely had
a restraining order against them, so they had been removed
from their home and couldn't leave the state. These were open
groups, which meant people were starting and finishing at
different times, versus a closed group, where all people begin
and end at the same time. Needless to say, people entering the

group did not want to be there and were quite angry at first. As the new people would defensively come into the group, the existing members had already settled in.

When men entered their men's only group, I found it would take them between four and six meetings until they let their guard down. Until then, they were blaming the system, blaming their partner—just angry. They were curt and emotionally shut down. The older members seemed to have patience with the new, attitude-filled guys because they had been there themselves a few months prior.

When the women entered their women's only group, they were usually a little guarded the first meeting but would quickly settle in. They felt validated and accepted by the existing women and appeared ready to learn about anger and toxic relationships. It seemed they were eager to learn ways to find their happiness.

Seeing the consistent difference between the men and women made me sad sometimes because, as a society, women are encouraged to sit around and talk about our feelings. Men, on the other hand, tend to feel demasculinized, weak, and defective when talking about vulnerable emotions. They don't sit around and talk with each other until they are forced to do so, and that is when I had the opportunity to work with them. I'll tell you one thing. At the end of the thirty-six weeks together, several men had made connections with each other that I could see lasting outside of the group. Many men didn't want to leave the group, and some even stayed and attended on a voluntary basis.

I wish our society embraced acknowledging emotions and promoted mental health awareness. I could get on my soapbox about society's stigma around mental health, but back to the Cone of Fear. So, once the men in my groups would let their guard down, it wasn't long before I saw tears. Tears about their past, tears about trauma they had endured, or the guilt they felt about the pain they had caused their partners or their kids. Soon, we would whittle all this down to the real, raw emotion of fear.

So, I ask, is it really better to stay guarded and protect the vulnerable aspects of ourselves? I'd say 99.9 percent of the domestic violence group members thought so until their anger resulted in legal issues. Only then did they find an opportunity to break through into the realm of what was behind those negatively expressed behaviors they displayed.

Back to the diagram. The top layer symbolizes all the negatively expressed emotions to keep people guarded and protected. Protected from what, you ask? The very next layer under the projected emotion is like a thick slab of concrete separating the defensive side of us and the vulnerability that lies bubbling underneath. If you drill holes through the concrete, you will find the emotions that make us feel—*really* feel. You begin to sift through some sadness or depression. Next, you reach into some worry and anxiety. Keep digging and you uncover guilt, and then, even deeper is shame. At the very bottom of the cone, the vortex of all the emotion, you will find fear. You can narrow fear down to two main sources, the fear of being rejected and the fear of being abandoned. However, who wants to feel all of that? Most of us do not buy tickets for that train. No way. Instead, we protect this core of emotion using the negatively expressed emotions that keep our fears locked away.

It seems like the more guarded and angrier a person is, the more fear they have stored away in the depths of their mind. I have a married couple I see for joint counseling; I will call them Sophie and Dan. Dan attends therapy because Sophie is telling him she's leaving if he won't come. Dan hates coming to my office. He interrupts me as I talk, he counters every idea I have, and he balks each time I ask him to explain an emotion. At about the time I was feeling hopeless to help Sophie and Dan, it hit me. There was so much pain and suffering inside Dan, and he had been hiding behind his anger for a long time.

I began offering him some guiding statements to see if I could validate some emotions. I said things like, "Dan, that must have been so confusing growing up with your mom having boyfriend after boyfriend and not knowing who was staying and who was leaving." He would nod.

I would continue, saying, "Dan, I'd imagine you felt left out and pretty disconnected from your mom. Maybe even feeling like she was choosing these boyfriends over choosing you." Dan would start shifting around from his side of the couch.

Pretty soon, he started elaborating about how lonely he was as a child. He hated being at home. His mom and the boyfriends would drink and do drugs. He recalled being so scared one time when his mom was passed out and he couldn't wake her up. Dan even started to tear up when he recalled this traumatic event. Tears were an emotion I never thought I would see from him, but sure enough, we were starting to get into the real feelings. I was seeing the vulnerability that Dan was terrified to display. Therapy finally began right them. Now, we could actually address some fears that Dan carried around but was too proud to admit. Or possibly, these fears were so buried that he never really made a connection. The catacombs of his mind were so riddled with fears of rejection and abandonment that he taught himself to reject others before they could reject him. He connected with the idea of, "I'll hurt you before you can hurt me." That is why Sophie felt so lonely in the marriage.

Understanding the Cone of Fear is a gateway to finding your peace. Whether you are learning about what drives your negative emotions or if you are taking someone else's hurtful behavior on as your own, I encourage you to use this tool and peel away the layers. I challenge you to recognize any awful, mean, cruel action that is externally expressed by someone, and I will guarantee you the root leads all the way to a fear. Fear of rejection. Fear of abandonment. Accept the challenge?

CREATING YOUR NON-NEGOTIABLES

Why not decide right here, right now, what you want for yourself in life. How do you know if you are compromising if you never set up any expectations? Developing a list of what you want in your job, in a relationship, in romance, will assure you are respecting yourself to the highest degree. Did you realize that up to this point in this book, you have been slowly learning what your non-negotiables look like? All of the past sections of this book sought to help you analyze yourself and your past in order to help you discover what is important to you. You have been laying the groundwork. The lessons here are helping you understand the significance of your past and helping you take part in creating what you want as you move forward in your life. Take action now to develop a list of what you will set in stone and never settle for less. You're about to make a contract with yourself that will honor your worth.

MODULE 4- CONFLICT MANAGEMENT STYLES

AVOIDANT

PEACEKEEPER

MY WAY OR THE HIGHWAY

COLLABORTOR

COMPROMISER

Go back to the timeline you created of past relationships. Use this diagram to brainstorm all the aspects of what made you content and fulfilled and what made you dissatisfied and sorrowful. After you have spent a few minutes jotting down anything that comes to mind, group similar elements together. For example, if laughing until you snort, cracking up, and joking around are on your list, you can categorize this as humor. Here, humor is a non-negotiable in your romantic relationship. Get creative with your list, and don't worry about creating a mile-long list. We will talk about that in a bit. For now, let the creativity flow. Here are some possible qualities in a relationship you might put on your non-negotiable list to get you started.

- Respect

- Commitment

- Feeling appreciated

- Trust

- Humor

- Passion

- Connection to their family or the ability to connect with your family

- Financial stability

- Career-oriented

- Intellectual compatibility

- Future goals that are in sync with your own

- Loyal

- Emotionally supportive

- Empathetic

You can start here and make this personal to you. If these characteristics were present in your relationship, would you be fulfilled? What would it look like? How are these points demonstrated? Are you showing up actively in these areas? If not, what do you need to do to exhibit what it is you want from someone else?

I hear you screaming, "There is no way a person with all these characteristics actually exists outside of Matthew McConaughey." (Okay, yes, he's my fave.)

You are partially correct. No one is perfect. I'm sure even Matthew has some flaws behind that sexy smile. But if you live your life guided by the list of non-negotiables you created, why would you think you deserve anything less? If something made it onto your list, you owe it to yourself to make it a priority in your life. Otherwise, you are basically telling yourself you don't deserve it. Might as well scoop out a piece of your confidence and sling it to the floor.

I have a client I saw a few years ago whom I'll call Andi. Andi didn't believe she would ever find a good guy. She felt like she was a magnet for the lying, cheating kind of guy. She was attracted to the challenge, the bad-boy type. There was something radiant about a tatted-up man on a motorcycle, *come-get-me eyes* peering at her over his shades—understandably so. Andi was beautiful, had a heart of gold, was successful in her career, and felt like her life was on track, except when it came to love. Her average relationship lasted about three years, just long enough for her to really get her heart invested, start making some long-term plans, and then, bam, his true colors would present themselves, and he'd be out the door.

In hindsight, the blazing red flags were very obvious, but in the moment, they were camouflaged by her idea of who she was falling in love with (as opposed to the man himself). Despite Andi's right-on-track type of life at the age of thirty-eight, her confidence was taking a toll as she described herself as an old spinster.

We started talking about what she wanted in a romantic relationship. She'd always jumped in headfirst and hadn't ever thought about making a list of her non-negotiables. But after spending some mental energy picking apart her past relationships, she used the timeline and was able to create a list of what was important to her. She described how she wanted to be treated, how she wanted a person to show up for her, how she wanted to spend holidays and vacations, what interactions would be like with this future man she hadn't met yet. Andi was able to see where she had been compromising herself in every relationship. She felt she'd been asking too much of someone else if she wanted them to treat her with complete respect and admiration. Because Andi didn't think she deserved as much, she made excuses for the men she dated when they treated her as less than. She personalized her desires and chalked it up to living in the real world and not in a Hollywood film production.

Andi summarized her list onto a piece of paper, folded it up, and kept it in her wallet, right behind her most used credit card. Every time she had to pull out the card, she would see her list and say to herself, "I deserve nothing less." By ingraining this into the core of her being, Andi began believing that she wasn't asking too much for a person to show up in the way she wanted them to. It wasn't too much later that Andi started dating again, and she immediately noticed the quality of men she was attracting had improved dramatically.

I recently heard from her. She sent me a text message with a picture of her wedding invitation and the worn-out piece of paper she'd written her non-negotiables on and carried around with her. She didn't compromise herself and found her Mr. Forever.

Meeting a person who measures up to what you deserve is all about timing and energy. You can't force this to happen or plan that on February 20, at 5:46 p.m., while choosing which avocados you'll buy at the grocery store, you will meet the man of your dreams. It doesn't work that way. However, if you know in your heart of hearts what you are looking for, and you show up in your life honoring each of those characteristics, you portray a certain energy. Why? Because you are confident. You know what you want, you know what you will not tolerate, and you will not accept anything less. You put out an energy that emits self-respect, and you require that from other people.

Can you recall the last crummy relationship you were in? What type of emotional space you were in when you attracted that person? Most times, that space is described as the bad-relationship-is-better-than-no-relationship type. Watch out because that is exactly what you're attracting. It's as if you have a blindfold on, playing Marco Polo, calling out for someone to date you. What happens is that you will likely attract someone who also has their blindfold on, just wishing for anyone to date. And there you go. It doesn't have to be like that. You can have so much more control over the quality of people you attract just by honoring and respecting yourself.

Still thinking this is too good to be true? I want you to try this experiment. Next time you go out, to the store, to the office, to a restaurant, change your body language in a way that does not promote connection with others. For example, before you walk out of the house, tell yourself some really critical things about yourself. (I know. It's so counterintuitive to what this book is really encouraging. But you know you do it sometimes anyway, so just roll with me for a minute.) So, here you are, ready to leave your house, and you tell yourself you look terrible. Now, you're driving, and you are criticizing other drivers.

Once you reach your destination, criticize how you parked and head on into the facility. Don't make eye contact with people, throw a smug look on your face, and slouch your shoulders. Ugh, just writing this makes my insides go all wonky. But try it if you don't think energy has anything to do with attracting people. Notice how you feel. Notice how others treat you. Anyone hold the door for you or say, "Excuse me," or ask how your day is? How do you think you are making other people feel? Warm and loving or cold and gloomy?

Part two of the experiment. Different outing. Before you leave the house, tell yourself some positive, encouraging statements. (Great time for the coping statement you came up with earlier.) Take a deep breath, get in your car, and drive to your destination. Listen to upbeat music or an inspiring podcast on your way. Allow people to merge in front of you and wave to people who let you get in front of them. Once you reach where you're going, take a deep breath before you get out of the car and say a few more encouraging statements to yourself. Now, enter the facility, shoulders down and back, head high, making eye contact with people, allowing yourself to smile. How are people reacting to you now? How many people said hello? How many people smiled back at you? How many people asked how your day was going and maybe even started a conversation with you? It's your energy. You either attract people, or you push them away. When you are out there in the dating world, meeting potential partners, what do you want your energy to say? *Yes, I am confident, I respect myself, and I will not compromise what is important to me in my life.*

WHEN TO COMPROMISE

Too much of a good thing is not a good thing. Chocolate is delicious, but too much chocolate will make you sick. Exercise is a good thing, but too much exercise will result in harming your body. It's the same with your non-negotiables. If you set your standards too high or are unaware of why you set them as you did, you may fall short of the mark every time. Many of my clients do not know where that line should be drawn and second guess the items on their list.

Being in a relationship with another person means that you can't always have things your way all the time. I saw a client named Shelly, age forty-three. Shelly was a serial dater. She always had first dates, sometimes had second dates, and rarely ever had a third date with the same guy. She'd etched her non-negotiables in stone and refused to deviate away from her list. She didn't have any serious relationships to put on her timeline, so we used her perception of her friend's relationship and her sister's marriage, and we even chose some relationships from her favorite movies.

What Shelly realized was that she had to compromise in some areas. Before we went through her non-negotiables and compromised on a few of them, we discovered she was clinging to very unrealistic and unnecessary qualities—for instance, she would only date men who made over $200,000 a year. She wanted someone who had multiple properties and loved to travel. She wanted to date someone who had never been married and didn't have any kids. Her perfect match was someone who liked to golf. She hated camping and hiking but liked to relax on the beach with a cocktail. While this imaginative person may exist, Shelly's list didn't consider any character attributes. There was nothing on her list about trust or honesty or empathy. Shelly was attracting men who were emotionally unavailable and not interested in anything long-term or serious.

She looked to the material aspects to make her feel secure and important in a relationship but was slowly learning that without seeking the foundational aspects, she was setting herself up for an emotionally empty connection, and that's what she was finding. While there were some things she was unwilling to compromise around (like a partner already having kids), she could compromise on her partner having been married in the past. Shelly realized that a fear was that if her partner had been previously married, she wouldn't be his number one. This had more to do with trust and commitment, and she was worried a previously married partner would likely go back to his ex. Building her confidence up and strengthening her ability to trust were issues that Shelly had to work on, rather than something to do with the other person.

Shelly found she was also willing to compromise on some of the material aspects. As she looked deeper into this, she wanted someone who was financially stable. Growing up, Shelly was one of eight children. Her parents worked hard, but they never had enough food, and she never had a new dress to wear: all her clothes had been handed down to her after her three older sisters had worn them out. Shelly had learned to equate money with stability.

As we picked apart certain unrealistic or overly particular items on her non-negotiable list, we discovered there was always a deeper reason behind them, and by evaluating those reasons, Shelly learned a lot about herself. She realized she had dependency issues and relied on other people to give her reassurance that she would be okay physically, emotionally, and mentally. She also realized that her strict and highly specific list kept her from falling in love and opening her heart: she was afraid and used her list as a protection to avoid getting hurt. By improving Shelly's confidence, we made it possible for her to develop a list of non-negotiables that would promote a healthy, loving relationship.

Do you remember when we talked about compromising as a way to resolve conflict? It meant that sometimes you have to give in, and that is okay. As you develop your list of non-negotiables (things you are not willing to compromise on), also develop a second list of negotiables (things that are important to you but that you *are* willing to compromise on). Shelly was able to shift some items from her non-negotiable list over to the negotiable list. These items weren't complete deal-breakers, although she felt they'd be nice for her to have as part of the relationship. Some items that were on her negotiable list were that her partner could have been married in the past, but she wanted to learn more about that relationship and feel reassured that it was truly over and her partner had successfully moved on. Another item was that her partner would like to hike and camp. He could go do those activities as his buddy time because she didn't have to be with him all the time. They could have separate interests, even traveling to different types of places, but it was important to her to have similar interests as well. So, *Similar Interests* made the non-negotiable list, while *hiking*, specifically, did not.

Make your list of non-negotiables and refer back to it periodically. It's always easier to make your list *before* you meet someone because you're less likely to make excuses for places where they may not measure up. For example, if you meet your Matthew McConaughey type, but he is $180,000 in debt and has no intention to pay it off, and you haven't made a list with "financially stable" on it, you may throw caution to the wind and say, "Financial stability is not that important," because whatever, he's a Matthew McConaughey type. Oops, don't do that!

SELF-REFLECTION

Okay, you beautiful soul, now it's time to do the work. Here is your list of what to do for yourself.

- Create your timeline of past relationships.

- Answer all the questions we discussed as it pertains to your past relationships.

- Draw your own Cone of Fear and fill out what the defensive actions look like to you. What negatively expressed behaviors are you aware of that you project? What do you notice in people close to you?

- Identify areas in the vulnerable section of the cone. What makes you sad, anxious? What are you feeling guilt and shame about? What are some deep fears around rejection and abandonment? Do you have fears around success or failure? What about the people you are attracted to? How would you fill out this cone for them? Do you see them differently now? What work do you need to do to feel more emotionally prepared to date?

- Create your list of non-negotiables and your list of negotiables. Group similar aspects together and understand your intention for each aspect. Is it realistic? Are you setting yourself up to succeed or to fail?

CHAPTER 8:
Ready, Set, Launch!

OKAY, MY LOVELY, I hope you can take a step back and realize the work you have done so far. Up to this point, you have gotten your mind right and put some structure into your life.

You have identified what Family Roles you gravitate toward and gained insight into why you are attracted to certain people.

You have learned about Attachment Style and which Personality Type you relate to, which helps you understand how you communicate and manage conflict in negative situations.

You have worked to improve your confidence and found forgiveness in painful areas of your life that were keeping you emotionally stuck.

You have also completed a timeline of your past relationships and gained knowledge of why the relationships ended, what lessons you learned, and what red flags were present so you can build from past experiences and choose partners who are healthier for you in the future.

In addition, you have developed your list of non-negotiables and committed to showing up in your life in a way that will not compromise your level of self-worth. In doing so, you have set firm, realistic expectations of how others show up in your life. By your achieving this level of self-respect, others around you won't have any choice but to also honor you in the highest regard.

Before you go out into the jungle and cast your net, this chapter will explain how you can create and maintain the foundation of a healthy relationship. We will discuss the difference between healthy and toxic intimacy and define your inspection checklist.

FOUNDATION OF A RELATIONSHIP

> "It's not the beauty of a building you should look at; it's the construction of the foundation that will stand the test of time."
>
> **—David Allan Coe**

MODULE 7- FOUNDATION OF A RELATIONSHIP

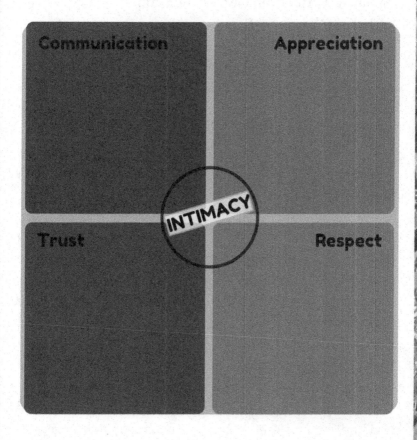

Communication

Appreciation

INTIMACY

Trust

Respect

Though this book focuses on romantic relationships, you may have noticed that the lessons you have learned in its pages can be applied to any relationship, including a neighbor, a boss, a colleague, a family member, or a dear friend—not just a romantic relationship. The diagram you see here of the foundation of a relationship is no different. The four squares must be stable and strong within the relationship. No matter what, you must have a solid base established before you can grow and deepen a connection with anyone. The center circle, intimacy, is what separates a romantic partnership from the relationship with the guy who sacks your groceries. (Unless, of course, he is your romantic partner, but you get what I'm saying.) Let's begin to dissect.

Communication, Appreciation, Trust, and Respect. These methods of connection are crucial to building healthy relationships with people. If any of these four factors are compromised, you will immediately notice how your defenses fly up in order to protect yourself. In fact, in the last chapter when you created your non-negotiables, I would guarantee that these four words made it onto your list in one form or another. (If they didn't, go back and reread this book because I think you overlooked a concept or two.)

As you see, the four areas of the foundation are divided by a line, but they are not separate from each other. Instead, they all work together like the gears in a clock. As one turns, it forces the next gear to turn, which is connected to another gear. When one gets blocked, it affects the rest of the gears, and pretty soon, the clock shuts down.

In terms of a romantic relationship, when all four aspects of the foundation are connected, intimacy is at its strongest. However, when one or more of these factors are damaged, intimacy is usually the first thing to leave a relationship, and it can be the last thing to come back. That is why the concept of intimacy is in the center, joining all four squares but also needing all four to be complete. Intimacy has many layers. Yes, having great sex is one layer, but intimacy is also snuggling on the couch, holding hands while walking into Costco, touching toes in bed before you fall asleep.

You might be asking why intimacy is the first factor to diminish in romantic relationships. It's because intimacy requires a deeper vulnerability, and to be vulnerable, you must feel comfortable and safe. Some people feel it's easy to have sex with someone but more difficult to have a deep conversation with them. However, that is just the act of having sex, void of a meaningful connection with another person. This is again why intimacy requires vulnerability.

Let's talk about sex. It is such an important factor in a romantic relationship, but many people don't see that if it's not nurtured and cherished, sex will become a tangled bunch of twine. When sex becomes complex, you know, when it's all about how many times a week or month you didn't have sex, or who's initiating and who's not. Or when sex becomes nonexistent. When this happens, people think that is when their relationship fell apart. But I am here to tell you that relationship crumbled a long time ago. When most couples come to see me and fill out the "Goals of Therapy" on their intake form, the most common problem they write down is that they no longer have sex. After I talk with these couples about this foundation of a relationship concept, it then becomes clear why sex became absent in their relationship. Neither partner felt respected or appreciated and noticed that their communication was based in negativity. Generally, men tend to feel their relationship is solid if their sex life is frequent and active. Women tend to feel their relationship is solid if they are connecting emotionally with their partner. Sex is important to both people, but looking at it from each angle, the need for all four areas to be strong is what brings them together intimately. Otherwise, the brokenness divides them.

Have you ever been in a relationship with someone, and it seems like all you do is argue over the stupidest, most unimportant things? You feel like you are a hamster in a wheel, running and running, totally out of breath but not getting anywhere. The argument goes in circles, picking up more tangents and items to throw into the mix, but there's still no resolution. Oh, it is exhausting and completely unproductive.

Time to throw up the stop sign. It might be necessary to take a Time-Out and collect your thoughts. After the Time-In, and after validation and clarification have taken place, it's time to have a dialogue about the issues at hand. What you will likely find is that it wasn't ever really about not putting the dirty dishes into the dishwasher or leaving the laundry in a wrinkly pile after taking it out of the dryer. No, the argument isn't really about the specifics, which are just surface-level issues.

When you get stuck on these surface-level situations, you start to recall all the other situations that make you angry. You have just jumped back onto the hamster wheel. It is important to take note of these detailed situations, but I suggest making a note of those in your mind first. Then you can categorize them and anchor them down into the four foundational aspects. Constantly picking up after your partner is more about feeling disrespected and unappreciated. You could say, "I feel disrespected and unappreciated when I have spent time cleaning the kitchen only to find your dirty dishes in the sink."

If, instead, you start the conversation by telling your partner, "Why can't you just put your dirty dishes in the sink?" you may end up with responses like, "I was going to do it later. Why are you always nagging me?" or "Well, why can't you clean your hair out of the bathroom sink?"

And there is your ticket to hamster-wheel land. What happened in this conversation is that you lost your focus and offered a platform for both of you to aimlessly vent your gripes. You began the conversation with a criticism, likely based on perspective. The defense from your partner went up, and he fired back. The conversation began with each of you being on two totally different pages.

However, when you can mentally nail your gripe down to a foundational aspect and work from a place of respect, appreciation, trust, or communication, the conversation will be more productive. See, when you begin the conversation saying, "I feel disrespected when..." you are connecting using the word respect, a foundational aspect that is hopefully important to both of you in the relationship. So, you start out on the same page instead of two different perspectives about one situation. When starting with one of the four squares, you'll find progress in the discussion because you are starting from the end goal, which in this case is respecting each other.

Trust, in the initial sense, may be defined as not cheating on your partner. However, another huge facet of trust is the need to create a trusting atmosphere. That includes creating a space within the relationship where you can be yourself, talk about the difficult things, even lose your mind over something, and know that you are still accepted. This is the ability to be your raw self and because there is trust, your partner isn't headed out the back door. Please don't confuse having a trusting environment and being your raw self with being vicious and wicked. Trust is a two-way street. By allowing and creating trust, each partner is conscious of the other person's emotions. Getting angry and having conflict is normal, but having trust is knowing that line of cruelty which you will never cross because you care so deeply for your partner. Having trust is the ability to have healthy conflict.

Deb and Ron, a couple I counsel, have been married for about seven years, and they have a two-year-old son together. On the verge of separation, they have come to counseling in a last attempt to make the marriage work. Deb struggles with anxiety, which presents as anger and irritation. Ron comes from a family where people constantly yell at each other, and he shuts down when Deb yells. Imagine what that does to Deb's anxiety when Ron tunes her out. Notice the hamster wheel they get into. The more Deb gets angry at Ron, the more she throws accusations, talks in a demeaning tone, and interrupts him. Trust is violated, and more problems are created. Deb's anger isn't rooted in issues with Tom. They are rooted in her fears of not being heard, being dismissed, being rejected. Tom is unaware of what is driving Deb's anger, and he shuts down because he gets so overwhelmed. I am helping them understand the dynamic they have created and teaching them the tools to create a trusting atmosphere that will encourage a more rewarding dialogue.

Deb's and Ron's lack of trust is related to a lack of healthy communication, which is the fourth factor of the foundation. As I have stated, the communication portion makes up the majority of what a relationship is built on. Think of communication as an umbrella, and under the umbrella are the components of communication: tone, presentation, body language, and the biggest one, resolving conflict. Encouraging someone to engage in a conversation requires a warm invitation. You are saying, "Hey, I really want you to hear what I am saying and what I am needing." If your approach is intimidating and inspires fear, the invitation will likely be declined or met with a matching negative stance. Conversation over.

Deb is working on using joining words and statements such as, "Let's work through this together," and "We can be a team and figure this out." Ron seems to open up because he feels talked with and not talked at. Not only is communication now more effective, but he also feels more respected, and as they work through their issues, Deb feels more appreciated. Overall, the trust is increasing because the defenses are going down. When they sit on my couch together, they don't automatically put the pillows in between them as they did for the first few sessions. Instead, they sit closer together. A sign that intimacy is finding its way back into the relationship.

A relationship is like a dance. The music, the steps, the rhythm; they all must work together. Sometimes the dance that people create in their relationships can be toxic, but they keep on dancing. They disregard the fact that they step on each other's toes, drop each other when one leans too close, but the music goes on, and so do they. Dresses become tattered, and shoes fall apart until they are a mess out there on the floor. Other dancers flow like willow trees in a soft wind. They are aware of their dance partners, they take breaks when they're out of breath, they have healthy space when appropriate, but they also hold each other close. The music is appealing, the dance is entrancing, and the connection is unmistakable. It is because all five areas of the foundation are intact.

SELF-REFLECTION

I challenge you to use the diagram of the foundation. First, define what each area means to you. For example, when you feel respected, what is going on? What do you need from your partner to feel respected? Answer these questions for the appreciation, trust, and communication categories.

Next, on a separate piece of paper, take a few minutes and vent. Make a list of irritations and resentments you have about a current or past relationship. Evaluate each aspect and identify which category in the foundation you can place each gripe. Does it fall under the category of respect, appreciation, communication, or trust? Have you ever thought about these situational aspects having a deeper root?

After you do this exercise, you may feel less rattled inside. You may feel a sense of direction because now you see the root element. Now, you can focus on the bottom-line issue instead of getting caught up in the hamster wheel. "Aha," you say, "I'm picking up what you're laying down." Makes sense, right?

Want to take this exercise to a deeper level?

Use the diagram of the foundation, but now associate a color with each square. For example, when I think of respect, I see blue. Trust is green. Appreciation is yellow, and communication is pink.

Now on a separate piece of paper, draw a figure of yourself. Not a stick figure, but a full-body picture. When I do this, my drawing looks like it was created by a five-year-old who is just learning to draw, but who cares, just draw it.

Take another piece of paper, turn it sideways, and draw a horizontal line from the left side, all the way to the right. The line you have drawn will be a timeline on which you will record your past memories of respect, trust, appreciation, or communication being violated, with the earliest date on the far left end of the line and today's date on the far right end.

Set your timer for three minutes. Start with your first color and square—for instance, blue for respect—and recall the many times you remember being disrespected, in whatever way comes to mind, placing it on the timeline in chronological order. Write in blue marker what that situation involved that made you feel disrespected at that particular time in your life. For example, I remember a relationship I was in, and my boyfriend at the time would talk about our intimate details to his roommate in front of me. They would laugh and tease me, but I never thought it was funny and felt incredibly disrespected. I'd embarrassingly laugh along, but I was dying inside, not strong enough to set a limit. So, I would write this in blue marker on my timeline around age twenty-one.

When the timer dings, get your next color, set the timer, and repeat. Do this for all four colors. Jot down on your time-line when you felt a lack of trust, appreciation, and communication gone sideways. Don't forget to set the timer. Again, this can be triggering, so if you feel overly anxious at any time, stop and move to part two of this exercise.

When you are finished recalling events and writing them on your timeline, you will see a rainbow of life that you have reflected on. Bits and pieces of yourself will be scattered all over the place on the sheet of paper in front of you.

Take a deep breath and remember the coping statement you came up with in Chapter 6. "I have worth," or "I don't have to prove myself to anyone," or "I deeply and completely accept myself." Whatever coping statement you choose, now is a good time to repeat it out loud.

Next, take the blue, the red, the yellow, and the green colors that make up your timeline and fill in your entire body drawing. You are gathering back your missing pieces. Recall where in your body you felt disrespected, where you felt unappreciated, where you felt trust was violated, and where you felt verbally abused. Collect all of those instances and retrieve what was unfairly taken from you. Collect the broken shards of colorful glass scattered all over the place to create a beautiful kaleidoscope within yourself. Fill up your body figure drawing with all of the colors of respect, trust, appreciation, and communication, making yourself a whole person again.

You may also look back at times you treated others poorly and have guilt or remorse. Learn from your lessons and choose to think and behave differently now moving forward. When you are finished with your timeline, look at your body and how all aspects of the foundation are gathered. You are complete, you are whole, you have worth. We all have a past, but how you organize it in your mind will determine if it drags you down or allows you to move forward with knowledge and confidence.

Be completely honest with yourself and ask if you treat others with total respect, trust, appreciation, and healthy communication. Think of this. If we all treated each other from this framework, what would our relationships be like? When we are not treating each other from this framework, our guard is up, and we are shutting down.

HEALTHY VERSUS TOXIC RELATIONSHIPS

In my early twenties, I read a book called *The Verbally Abusive Relationship* by Patricia Evans. It was recommended to me by my therapist, who was trying to help me see my way out of an extremely toxic relationship I was all wrapped up in. I knew in my heart that things weren't good with my partner, but I knew the dance steps by heart, and it was hard to break the habit. I guess I listened to that little internal voice enough to get into counseling, so there I sat, week after week, deciding if I was ready to leave him.

When I read this book, I realized that it wasn't so much the educational aspects and how-to's that stood out; it was the actual quotes of a verbally abusive person that glared at me from each page. I could visualize my partner saying these exact words, and I was astonished—I felt as if the author were speaking directly to me. It was then that I realized I was stuck in an abusive relationship. Weird, isn't it, how everything around you can be so obvious, but we choose to ignore it until that one point in time when something leaps out and lands on our faces, that we finally have that aha moment?

Oprah Winfrey popularized the term "aha moment." The term became used so often and so universally that, in 2012, Merriam-Webster included it in the dictionary for the first time, ahead of "bucket list" and "sexting."

Here's what Oprah says about it: "You can't have an 'aha' unless you already knew it. So, the aha is the remembering of what you already knew, articulated in a way to resonate with your own truth. So, the aha isn't somebody teaching you something; the aha is somebody helping you to remember."

This section may be that time for you. Seeing on paper what a healthy and toxic relationship looks like may help you re-evaluate your own situation. As you may have discovered, based on the past chapters and learning about how you grew up, you may not have had the best examples demonstrated to you about what a healthy relationship looks like. You were forced to teach yourself these aspects, from the framework you know, and as you know, we learn from our mistakes.

Sometimes seeing the words in black and white can be eye-opening. I've asked clients of mine to read this list and when they see aspects of what constitutes a toxic relationship, their mouths drop to the floor. What was common and comfortable to them was listed right here on the "Toxic Components" side. How about you? An "aha" opportunity as you read on? Here is a list of several descriptors in their toxic form and in their healthy form. I encourage you to take inventory of how often you experience a particular side.

MODULE 7- HEALTHY VS TOXIC RELATIONSHIPS

Toxic Components Components	Healthy
Obsessed with finding someone to love	Development of self as the first priority
Need for immediate gratification	Desire for long term contentment- relationship develops step by step
Pressuring your partner for sex or commitment	Freedom of choice, teamwork with same goal in mind
Imbalance of power	Balance and mutuality in the relationship
Power play for control	Compromise, negotiation, and taking turns at leading
Shut down of communication, especially if things are not working out	Sharing wants, feelings, and appreciation of what your partner means to you
Manipulation	Directness
Lack of trust	Appropriate trust
Attempts to change your partner to meet your own needs	Embrace each other's individuality
Relationship is based on delusion and avoidance of any negativity	Relationship deals with all aspects of reality
Relationship stays stuck, change is resisted	Relationship has fluidity and changes with natural life transitions
Expectation that one partner will fix all the problems	Both partners participate in their individual self-care and work together through conflict
Obsession with the other person's problems and feelings and wanting to fix it.	Loving non-attachment- healthy concern about the partner's well-being, growth, but knowing what you can control and what you have zero control over
Blaming yourself or your partner for problems	Problem- solving together
Being stuck in the cycle of unhealthy conflict.	Utilizing the cycle of healthy conflict

MODULE 7- HEALTHY VS TOXIC RELATIONSHIPS

Below are questions for you to think about and answer using the diagram above. I'd encourage you to also elaborate your responses in your journal. The more expansive and honest you can be with yourself, the more you will get out of this exercise.

As you read through these examples, what is running through your mind?

- Have you been in relationships that are descriptive of the left side?

- Which aspects on the left could be associated with Dependent Personality, Borderline Personality, and Narcissistic Personality?

- What non-negotiables can you take from this and add to your list?

- Which of these describe your own behavior? What is the *why* behind this action?

- How can you shift your behavior to be healthier?

- Which aspects could be anchored down to the foundational qualities of respect, communication, appreciation, and trust?

- Do you carry resentments based on any of the aspects on the left side? What can you do to work through these resentments and let them go?

- Do you need to find forgiveness in any of these areas? Remember, forgiveness is not saying a behavior was okay. Forgiveness is finding peace within yourself.

- If you are engaged with aspects on the toxic side, how can you set limits and healthy boundaries to shift toward the healthy side?

INSPECTION CHECKLIST

Congratulations! You are just about ready to get out there into the jungle. As you complete this book, know that as a human being, you are always a work in progress. Just because you read all of the pages, completed the exercises, reflected on your past, and used the tools I've shared with you to respect yourself more doesn't mean the work is over. As you venture out and meet potential romantic partners or use these techniques to strengthen your current romantic relationship, you will experience bumps and falls. You may even experience heartbreak. However, I hope you will see these situations as opportunities to implement all you have learned here. We fall, we break, we fail. But we also rise, we heal, and we overcome.

MODULE 7-
INSPECTION CHECK LIST

 Respect

 Morals/Values

 Self-Reflection

 Accountable for Actions

 Chemistry

 Trustworthy

 Energy

 Communication Skills

Attitude

Confidence

In Chapter 1, I asked you to answer these questions by reflecting on yourself. It's time to evaluate everything you have learned since you began this journey. Before you go back to see how you answered these questions, go through them and evaluate where you stand on these aspects now. As we have discussed, creating an empowering relationship with yourself is the first step to finding a healthy, loving relationship. Not only are these attributes important when evaluating a partner, they also serve as guidelines to how to conduct yourself.

Remember in Chapter 1 when we talked about being world class? You completed an exercise to check in and self-assess in several aspects. Now it is time to complete your inventory again. Are you showing up in your life world-class style now? Do you have high but realistic expectations for yourself? Not only is it time for you to answer these questions based on how you see yourself, but I have added additional journal prompts to use these ten areas to evaluate a potential partner:

Respect: How are you showing yourself respect? What can you do today to be more respectful to yourself? How does your partner respect themselves? How do they show you respect?

Self-reflection: What are your goals? What are your successes? Is your partner able to look in the mirror and evaluate their own behavior? Are they willing to accept constructive criticism, and are they willing to make changes to improve their lives?

Chemistry: Are you vibing with people around you? Do you draw people toward you or push people away? Are you physically and emotionally attracted to your potential partner?

Energy: Do you radiate positivity? Gratitude? Non-judgment? Or do you transmit an uninviting flow? Does your potential partner exude tenderness and trust?

Attitude: Are you optimistic, pessimistic, realistic? Is the glass half-full or half-empty? How about your potential partner? What is the attitude you are picking up? How does it make you feel?

Morals and values: Are you walking your walk and talking your talk? When self-reflecting, are you in line with your beliefs and living your life that way? Is your potential partner matching your morals and values? Can you comfortably ask them about their belief system? Remember, actions speak louder than words.

Accountable for actions: Do you sincerely apologize for what is yours to own? Do you hold others accountable? Does the potential partner do the same? If they demonstrate negative behavior but do not hold responsibility for their actions, I promise you they won't change this, and you can't change it for them.

Trustworthy: Do you follow through on commitments? Can people rely on you? Are you honest with yourself? Does the potential partner demonstrate trust?

What's their history? Do they have long-term friend-ships? Do they exhibit honesty?

Communication skills: Do you know your Communication Style? Are you aware when it is disconnected from the people around you? Are you able to adjust it in order to work with people? Are you shut down? How do you feel about conflict? What are you doing to be more effective in this area? Have you learned the potential partner's Communication Style? How have they managed conflict in the past? Are they open to listening to you, or do they interrupt?

Confidence: Do you know your worth? Do you emanate humility? Are you able to comfortably spend time alone? Is the potential partner confident? Needy, clingy, independent? Do they take control of their lives? Do they know their worth and show a sense of self-worth?

Think of the hard work you are doing now and have done in the past to work toward being a healthier person. Why would you want to be with someone who doesn't appreciate you for who you are? When you personally demonstrate all of these qualities that you are looking for in someone else, it's fascinating who shows up in your life. Remember, you can't change other people. You can communicate what your needs are, you can be assertive and point out areas where your needs are not being met, and you can manage conflict skillfully, but you can never make someone be who they are not. Attempting to do so will only leave you feeling empty.

I want to tell you about a woman I'll call Sandy. She was always reading books to help her feel more empowered. She learned how to find success in her career, as a single parent, and in her friendships. But Sandy always fell short of finding success in her romantic relationships. She had high expectations for herself, and she found a way to meet whatever goal she set. But Sandy was attracted to people who always required so much emotional work that they left her feeling responsible for their happiness. She fell into the trap of taking care of the men she was with.

She always said, "I already have two kids. Why would I want a man-child?" She spent most of her adult life in therapy, working through her past, her traumas, her confidence. I would remind her that she was the one who showed up every two weeks, implementing all the tools I taught her. I would ask her why she kept settling for men who didn't put that same level of effort into their own lives. Why would she want to be with men who didn't take the time or the steps to evaluate and improve each of these ten areas listed above, as she was doing for herself?

As women, we tend to have higher expectations for ourselves and make excuses for other people when they don't meet those expectations. We feel that placing our expectations on others is being high maintenance, demanding, and bitchy. But no. Voice your expectations. If others are unable to meet them, be thankful for their honesty and decide to stay or keep on truckin.' Do you want a challenge, a project, or are you ready to be with someone who matches your ability for self-reflection and change, someone to meet you where you are on your journey of complete self-love? The choice is yours, and I have full confidence that you will choose to honor yourself.

My wish for you is not only to have healthy expectations of yourself as you show up in your life but to have the same expectations for those whom you choose to invite into your inner circle.

Every moment, experience, person, place, emotion, all the good and all the bad, has brought you to this moment right here. It has molded and shaped you into who you are. Now, it is up to you to wrap your arms around all of these things and find the gratitude. Even the trauma, even the heartache, even the tears and pain. When you can hold yourself with love, you no longer need another person, but another person will become a bonus to who you already are. And you are enough.

I also want to say that I am grateful that you have shared this time to whole-heartedly work through the chapters of this book. Thank you for trusting me and allowing yourself to uncover the raw emotion that likely rose to the surface throughout your experience. As my gift to you, I invite you to join my Facebook group called Women's Empowerment Toolkit and to join the Women's Empowerment Toolkit Inner Circle. This Inner Circle is offered to women who have chosen to embark on the life-changing skills utilizing *Preparing for the Jungle*. Here you will find a safe environment to ask questions, share experiences and gain support from other inspiring women. Please send me a message letting me know you are part of the Jungle group, and I will allow you access.

Sending you light and love,
Tami

ACKNOWLEDGMENTS

TO MY KIDS, Zachary and Dylan, for teaching me to be imaginative and think outside the box. You encourage me to always follow my heart and never give up as that's what makes dreams come true.

To my forever partner, Jim, for showing me true, unconditional love. You are my rock and I can't thank you enough for believing in me.

To my family for always being there to support me no matter what my wild and crazy ideas are and how outside of the box they may seem. You are the best cheerleaders out there!

Lastly, I want to thank the thousands of clients who have trusted me with their deepest, most secretive parts of their lives. You have all been teachers to me in one way or another and without you, this book would not have come to fruition. I hope that by using your experiences, you can be examples for others to get Prepared for the Jungle.

Would you like to work together or dig a little deeper into your own unique situation? Here are a couple ways:

1. Please join our amazing, safe, and motivating Facebook group—Women's Empowerment Toolkit at https://www.facebook.com/groups/womensempowermenttoolkit/.

2. Here is an online course that follows this book closely. You will find this seven-module course located on the easy-to-navigate Teachable platform. I personally walk you through each module using over thirty videos and all of the downloadable worksheets used in this book. Here you will hear and experience how to personalize your path through the Jungle: https://healthyhealing.teachable.com/.

3. Visit my website and drop me a line. I'd love to hear what you thought about the book as well as your personal aha's: https://www.healthy-healing.net.

ABOUT THE AUTHOR

TAMARA KIEKHAEFER, LCSW, has operated a successful psychotherapy practice since 2002. She provides individual, family, and couples therapy around anxiety, depression, domestic violence, trauma, relationships, and empowerment. She has taught workshops and spoken on podcasts guiding people to gain awareness of what is not working in their lives while offering strategies to gain a sense of internal control.

Tamara is a certified yoga instructor and weaves concepts of holistic therapy into her clinical work. Offeringa body/mind/soul approach, she addresses every angle crucial for stability and peace.

Her first book provides hand-on tools required to work through the past, stabilize the present, and prepare for a loving relationship. Having experienced her share of heartbreak, Tamara's compassion with real life adds to the richness of her writing.

She finds her own tranquility spending time with her teenage boys, family, dogs, and the love of her life, Jim.